Kyriaki Papageorgiou
Olga Kokshagina

ENVISIONING THE FUTURE OF LEARNING
FOR CREATIVITY, INNOVATION AND ENTREPRENEURSHIP

DE GRUYTER

Irma Arribas
Visual Thinker

Acknowledgements

This book is the result of collaborative work conducted in the context of the VISION project, funded by the EU Erasmus+ Knowledge Alliance program (number 612537-EPP-1-2019-1-SI-EPPKA2-KA). The opinions expressed in this work are the responsibility of the authors and do not reflect the official opinion of the European Union.

The authors would like to thank the VISION consortium partners (see pages 202–205) and specifically highlight: Tim Jones for designing the methodological framework for inquiring into the future co-creatively; Michelle Brocco for facilitating the online collaboration using IdeasCloud; Beata Lavrinovica and Rajnish Tiwari for their topic-specific leadership and important contribution throughout; Carina Leue-Bensch, Irina Fiegenbaum and Dietmar Schlößer for sharing their insights from industry; Louise Pulford for linking research to broader networks and cross-sector conversations; Laura Bellorni, Frederic Arnoux, and Collette Menard for their invaluable support; Anna Bessant and Lucija Barisic for ensuring that our work reaches the right audiences; Ana Šajn for keeping everyone on track with her spreadsheets; Abdelhamid El-Zoheiry for his support and astute policy perspective; John Bessant and Steffen Conn for their mentorship and insights; Irma Arribas and Irene Sierra for the making the book come alive with its visual look and and interplay between text and images; and Steve Hardman for supporting the creation of this book in an open access format.

The authors would also like to express their appreciation to everyone who shared their vision of the future of learning through interviews and workshops during the project. These people are listed on pages 206–211.

CONTENTS

A READER'S GUIDE TO THE FUTURE OF LEARNING

This book is a guide for those navigating the changing landscape of learning. It is designed primarily for educators or education managers working within Higher Education Institutions (HEIs), as well as policy makers involved in drafting new educational initiatives or reforms, and stakeholders from the industry and society at large who are interested or engaged in activities that aim to enhance creativity, innovation and entrepreneurship (CIE) through education. We understand that some of our readers might be new to the CIE learning space, whereas others might have many years of experience in implementing CIE-related programs. By focusing on the ongoing changes and emergent trends already evidenced in CIE educational programs, we hope to provide a better understanding about the characteristics and challenges they pose and offer suggestions on how to tackle these considering the readers' specific context and circumstances.

The map of the future of learning portrayed in our book is built on the collective inputs of more than 250 stakeholders around the world, whom we engaged in different ways over a 2-year period in the context of the EU-funded VISION project.[1] These stakeholders included HEI representatives, educators, students, EdTech start-up founders, policy makers, regulatory bodies, consultants, practitioners and think tanks. The VISION project research team[2] conducted 130 one-to-one interviews and gathered a wealth of data describing different experiences, realities and visions about the future of learning. Once we began analyzing our material and extracting common themes, we organized eight online workshops with an average of 15 participants each, where we shared our findings and received feedback on our emerging view of the learning landscape. Additionally, we conducted four workshops involving key stakeholder groups separately (educators, policy makers, industry and students) to paint with finer strokes the learning landscape we are presenting here.

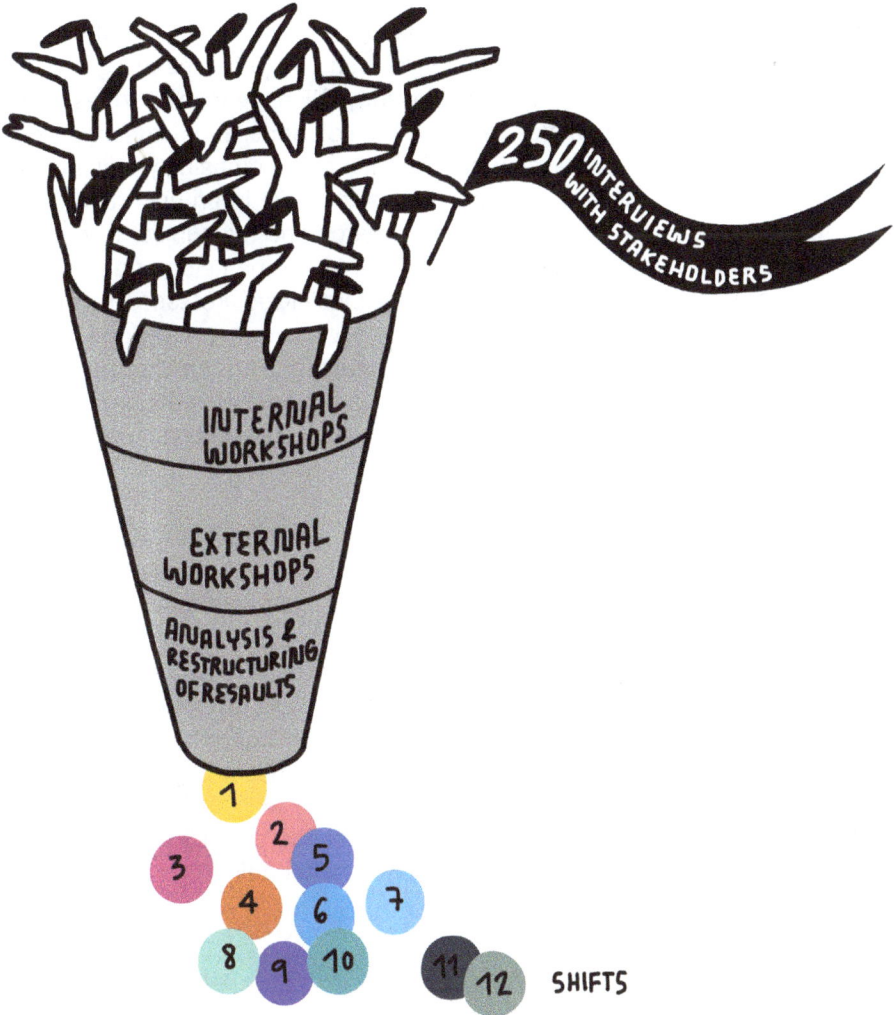

250 INTERVIEWS WITH STAKEHOLDERS

INTERNAL WORKSHOPS

EXTERNAL WORKSHOPS

ANALYSIS & RESTRUCTURING OF RESAULTS

1
2
3
4
5
6
7
8
9
10
11 12 SHIFTS

It is important to note that from the first stages of our research we realized that our interlocutors made little distinction between the future of learning *in general* and one that focuses on the future of learning for creativity, innovation and entrepreneurship (CIE). There are several reasons for this, all connected to the progressively prominent position these three intertwined competences are given within the broader socioeconomic landscape. Currently, CIE appear as priorities in policy documents, as essential qualities for business solutions, and as desired skills in work descriptions. They have been consistently and increasingly highlighted as critical for both individuals and organizations to thrive in an uncertain environment. CIE have become central topics of research and the subject of numerous academic papers; in some universities they have become fields or disciplines of their own, commanding new departments and specialized professorships. CIE are no longer only housed in business schools or exclusive to innovation managers, creative industry professionals and entrepreneurs, but are an integral part of a transversal set of skills relevant to learners of all ages across academia, industry, policy and society at large. In a nutshell, there is an overwhelming recognition that a future-ready landscape embeds learning for CIE.

A systematic analysis and comparison of the burgeoning CIE literature is beyond the scope of this book. Instead, we offer some broad definitions (see Table 1) and emphasize their interconnectivity and shared elements that are relevant to learning.[3] For example, new ideas are central across CIE, and consequently, mastering the process of generating these is pivotal. There is also great emphasis on the context within which ideas emerge and the kind of mindsets needed for cultivating CIE, such as taking risks and acting under conditions of uncertainty. Their commonalities are largely reflected in the existing learning programs, which tend to be more practical and hands-on than theoretical. Learning by doing plays a critical part in CIE, therefore training is grounded in practices that encourage students to *act* creatively, innovatively and entrepreneurially.

Table 1: Creativity, Innovation and Entrepreneurship

Creativity involves the skill (rather than the gift) of bringing about something new and valuable.[4]

Creativity is understood as the production of a novel and appropriate response, product, or solution to an open-ended task. As Teresa Amabile, a world-leading expert on creativity puts it: "Four components are necessary for any creative response: three components within the individual – domain-relevant skills, creativity-relevant processes, and intrinsic task motivation – and one component outside the individual – the social environment in which the individual is working."[5]

Innovation is defined "as the intentional introduction and application within a role, group or organization of ideas, processes or procedures, new to the relevant unit of adoption, designed to significantly benefit the individual, the group, organization or wider society."

Innovation is associated with the development of the product or practice of new and useful ideas to benefit individuals, teams, organizations or a broader range of society.[6]

Entrepreneurship relates to the discovery, evaluation and exploitation of opportunities in the process of business start-up, creation and growth; entrepreneurial dynamism is key to economic renewal and growth.[7] In most cases, entrepreneurship is seen as a tool for innovators to commercialize their innovations.[8] It is also understood as a way of thinking, acting and being that combines the ability to find or create new opportunities with the courage to act on them.[9]

The overall field of entrepreneurship is loosely defined as the creation of new business enterprises by individuals or small groups.[10]

Learning by doing, being in real-world environments and embracing experimenta-tion (and failure) were some of the characteristics repeatedly highlighted by our interlocutors as important for learning. Relatedly, the importance of more immer-sive and challenge-driven learning was emphasized. Readers with experience in teaching CIE will recognize these elements in their own work. But there are other characteristics raised in our research that are intimately interconnected to the above that are perhaps less obvious, such as the ways learners are evaluated and the impact that is expected from them at the end of their learning journey.

In this book we present 12 elements that make up what we call a "future-ready learning landscape." Taken together, these press against established education-al infrastructures and methods, making obvious the kinds of changes, or shifts needed in order to successfully deliver learning programs for CIE, now and in the future. We have organized the book in three parts:

PART I: Shifts in the learning landscape

This is the core part of our book. Each shift captures the transition and the movement that we have identified based on the interviews and workshops. You can be at the beginning of this transition or on your way. We see these changes happening across the education system as an opportunity to rethink how we cultivate learners and prepare them for the future.

PART II: Snapshots into the future

This captures how different organizations have already implemented these shifts in interesting and innovative ways. All the cases we present illustrate one or several shifts that are already happening within the traditional HEI sector, corporate or EdTech spaces. The main goal here is to illustrate how different organizations are embedding the shifts in their own learning landscape or helping others.

PART III: Creating a future-ready learning landscape

This offers guidance on how to revisit your own work and build on different tools and methods within CIE to think about the transition to a more engaging, personalized and future-ready learning journey. This part offers some concrete exercises that can help you better understand your current landscape and the kinds of changes you might need to implement to facilitate the transformation of the learning experiences you are currently leading and deliver the desired results for the learners.

PART I

SHIFTS IN THE LEARNING LANDSCAPE

This book uses the idea of shifts to discuss changes within the learning landscape. By shift we mean changes in position, direction or tendency that occur in the learning landscape from the traditional ecosystem to future-ready learning landscape. We use the idea of the learning landscape as a metaphor to map the abstract concept or learning into a physical journey that occurs in the real world. The future-ready learning landscape helps us to reflect on the shifts that will help education adjust to the needs of the future world of work, prepare learners and educators to navigate the changing ecosystem of learning.

We identified three groups of shifts and they are (a) pillars of learning, (b) learning journey and (c) learning results. The shifts examined in this book (see Table 2) demand the right tools and methods to ensure success for learners and teachers in their learning journey. We qualify the shifts by putting them in the context against the components of traditional education.

The shifts outlined in Part I aim to put learning back at the center of education and enable a more purpose-driven education by contributing to (a) develop mindful/responsible/skilled citizens, ready for life/the workforce/the future of work and (b) tackle big problems and grand challenges.

Importantly, we do not mean to imply that there is no room in the future of learning for elements or characteristics of established HEIs and traditional education. In many cases there are overlaps and elements are not completely erased, but emphasis is placed elsewhere. Our goal is to identify transitions while building on the existing elements of traditional education. Also, we need to acknowledge variations even within traditional education and that there are many pathways to change. In fact, HEIs are central, both as enablers of change, but also as recipients. The shifts presented next are evidence of this (see Table 2).

Table 2: Overview of Shifts

Element	Traditional education	Future-ready learning landscape
Pillars of learning		
Students	Passive and interim information recipients	Active and lifelong learners
Teachers	Lecturer and subject expert	Various roles: coach, mentor, facilitator, curator, practitioner, learning designer; continuous upskilling
Subject matter	Discipline-centered	Multidisciplinary, problem-based and challenge-driven
Spaces	Classrooms and lecture halls with fixed sitting	Flexible spaces and the real world
Learning journey		
Style	Individual and independent	Team-based and collaborative
Process	Linear	Iterative, exploratory and experimental
Physical material and other equipment	Backboards and textbooks	Arts and crafts
Digital technologies	One-directional	Interactive
Learning results		
Outputs	Written material	Written material, physical prototypes and action
Outcomes	Standardized knowledge acquisition	Personalized knowledge, skills and attributes
Impact	Institutional	Societal
Evaluation	One-dimensional	Multidimensional

1. PILLARS OF LEARNING	2. LEARNING JOURNEY	3. LEARNING RESULTS
TEACHER	STYLE	EVALUATION
STUDENT	PROCESS	OUTPUTS
SUBJECT MATTER	PHYSICAL MATERIAL ARTIFACTS	OUTCOMES
SPACE	DIGITAL TECHNOLOGY	IMPACT

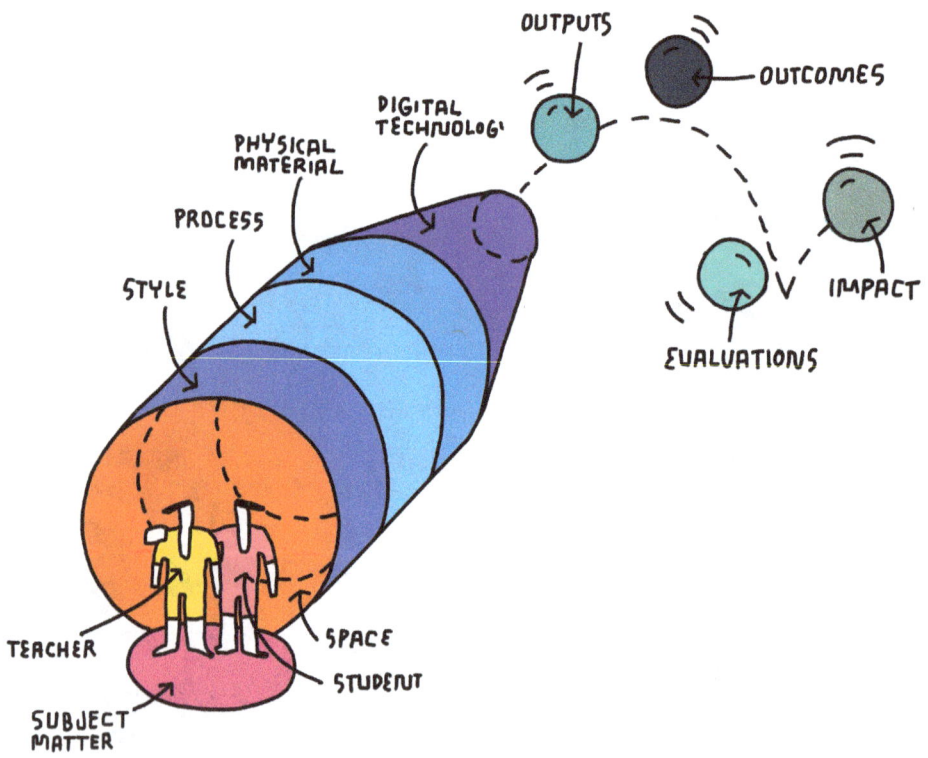

OUTPUTS

OUTCOMES

DIGITAL
TECHNOLOGY

PHYSICAL
MATERIAL

PROCESS

STYLE

IMPACT

EVALUATIONS

TEACHER

SPACE

STUDENT

SUBJECT
MATTER

PILLARS
OF LEARNING

Pillars of learning are foundational elements that serve as the basis of our educational systems. All educational systems need students, teachers, subject matter and spaces. Students are the recipients of the education system. Education needs to provide students with the navigation tools to find their own way through an increasingly complex and uncertain world. Therefore, the role of the teacher is critical. Though, it changes from expertise in content to expertise in facilitation, engagement and curation.

Today the challenge is to turn teachers into advanced knowledge workers with professional autonomy yet working in collaborative cultures. This also requires changes in the subject matter. Teaching and disciplines are largely divided by subject, but we see that they need to be integrated where students are not separated from the real world during their learning experience. Powerful learning environments should be multidisciplinary, challenge and problem based. Spaces for learning need to reflect this, facilitate the need to create synergies and find new ways to enhance professional, social and cultural capital with the outside world.

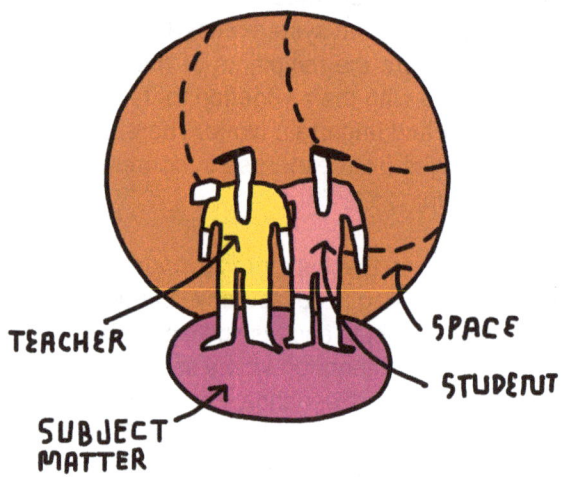

TEACHER

SPACE

STUDENT

SUBJECT
MATTER

1 Students: From passive and interim information recipients to active lifelong learners

Education is no longer optimized for an average student. Instead, it is transitioning to be student-centric, account for differences and preferences and to an extended definition of the learners of the future. Today's learners are increasingly multinational, wanting to make an impact on the world, and striving for a brighter future. They need to become experts in life-learning and not in one specific area.

2 Teachers: From lecturers and subject experts to coaches, curators, practitioners and learning designers

Being a lifelong learner applies to teachers as well. As an essential part of modern education, they need to have a positive approach when it comes to learning, be more flexible and open to new ideas and learning. Their role is changing from subject experts to coaches, facilitators, practitioners and even learning designers to reflect customized learning experience.

3 Subject Matter: From disciplinary-centered to multidisciplinary, problem- and challenge-based learning

Traditionally, teaching is disciplinary-centered and there is a lack of integration across disciplines. To suit the future needs, learning is becoming problem- and challenge-based where to tackle the real-world problems, a multidisciplinary approach is required. Teaching in the future needs to be more project based, building experiences that help students think across the boundaries of subject matter disciplines.

4 Spaces: From traditional classrooms and lecture halls to flexible spaces and the real world

Curriculum teaching and learning is already extending well beyond the classroom and will continue to do so, and as education changes to suit the future's needs. The learning is becoming more embedded in the real world and requires flexible spaces where learners can be immersed in their learning contexts.

1 STUDENTS: FROM PASSIVE AND INTERIM INFORMATION RECIPIENTS TO ACTIVE LIFELONG LEARNERS

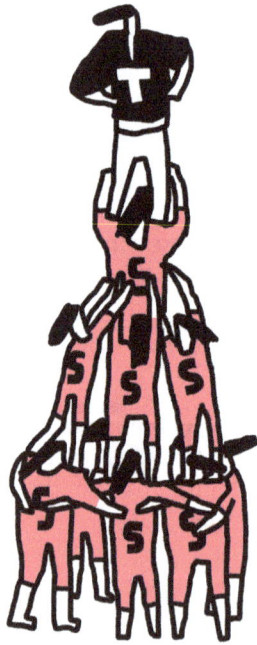

FROM
PASSIVE AND INTERIM
INFORMATION RECIPIENTS...

TO
ACTIVE LIFELONG LEARNERS

When one is asked to describe a student, the image that usually forms is that of a young adult sitting at a desk taking notes while a teacher is standing at the front of the classroom. Indeed, the traditional education framework places the student in the background as a listener and a passive receiver of information. The student is supposed to take notes during the class and usually has a textbook or a laptop that accompanies and further reinforces the information received. This information is discipline-oriented or subject specific, and normally connected to the students' chosen fields of interest. In due course, an exam is taken, or a research paper is delivered to assess the extent to which the knowledge transmitted was digested or recalled.

The goal was standardization and compliance, with students educated in age cohorts, following the same standard curriculum, all assessed at the same time. These students had the same tests or assignments on which they worked individually or in a group. At the end of the course the student receives a mark based on their performance in these assignments and to a lesser degree on class participation. Once successfully finishing a course, the student is allowed to carry on with more advanced courses on a similar topic, until they complete all the necessary requirements and collect the credits needed to graduate. And unless they chose to do a postgraduate course, they are no longer students but instead hopefully professionals in the workforce.

These are the familiar characteristics and trajectory of student life that are currently being challenged and considered inadequate for preparing them with the knowledge, skills and competences they need to successfully position themselves in the job market. Many initiatives are in place that produce a new kind of student that is better described as an active and lifelong learner. This is somebody who takes a hands-on and independent approach to learning, engages more deeply with the topic at hand and continues to study and learn beyond the institutional frameworks of a traditional degree.

One of the major consequences of this shift is the changing of roles and dynamics in the classroom. While in traditional education environments the teachers have complete authority over the learning process, the trend we have observed is to grant students greater agency, control and responsibility. Students are presented with options of what and how they study and they can largely self-direct their learning journey. Learning is based on student passions and capacities, helping students to personalize their learning and assessment in ways that foster engagement and helping them find their own pathway.

The goal is to help students learn and to give them the right tools to build on in the future. For example, in many CIE-related programs, students are presented with a set of methodologies for human-centered design, ideation and prototyping to help them decide who they would like to interview, what exactly they would like to create, why and how. They are given freedom as to how to approach and define the problem presented to them and thus pursue a subject or topic area that they are personally interested in. As they plan the evolution of their work and take responsibility for their actions, students learn how to learn and acquire a set of important life skills along the way, such as time management. Furthermore, students need to be able to outline their own vision for education,

> and it's shocking, in a way, because there are so many students everywhere. And one of the things that teachers do most is engage with students and yet, no one really asked us what we think about different teaching styles, because every student in the world could tell you what's the problem with legacy education. (Finn Macken, Student, Minerva)

Another important element to highlight in this shift is that learners become creators of knowledge or "epistemic agents."[11] This is particularly visible in the paradigm of challenge-based learning, where students must generate the knowledge needed rather than passively absorbing information presented to them. In fact, information needed for CIE is not readily available precisely because it embeds the personal passions, choices and interests of the students. Consequently, learners must collect and synthesize materials from diverse sources, including first-hand observations in the context they wish to make an intervention, as well as through interviews with users and other relevant experts.

While learners collaboratively bring together the bits and pieces of their data, they also connect an entire knowledge and innovation ecosystem and create, oftentimes unconsciously, their own learning infrastructure. According to Spence, "this is not an environment that is carefully crafted and provided by others to support a specific educational goal, but one that is 'achieved by the learners themselves' through 'organizing complexity and sense-making in unbound landscapes where intellectual, relational, material, or digital resources exist in abundance."[12] As a result, students are more deeply engaged, learning becomes more meaningful and whole, and perhaps most importantly, the skills and mindset for lifelong learning are acquired.

The shift from a student to a lifelong learner is critical in the face of the 21st-century labor market uncertainties, no matter the position or stage of one's career. In addition to professional survival and evolution, acquiring new skills, knowledge

and capabilities beyond the formal education years is important for the purpose of achieving personal fulfilment. When an individual decides to pursue personal interests and goals and become more knowledgeable on a specific topic, they also gain renewed self-motivation and self-confidence. Lifelong learners tend to have a growth mindset that defies statements such as "I will never" or "I am not capable of." Instead, they are characterized by curiosity, initiative, perseverance and imagination, and do not shy away from uncertainty and critique. Empowering individuals as lifelong learners begins in childhood, but it is never too late to alter established patterns of thought and behavior:

> *The illiterate of the 21st century will not be those who cannot read and write, but those who cannot learn, unlearn and relearn.* (Alvin Toffler)

2 TEACHERS: FROM LECTURERS AND SUBJECT EXPERTS TO COACHES, CURATORS, PRACTITIONERS AND LEARNING DESIGNERS

FROM
LECTURERS
AND SUBJECT EXPERTS...

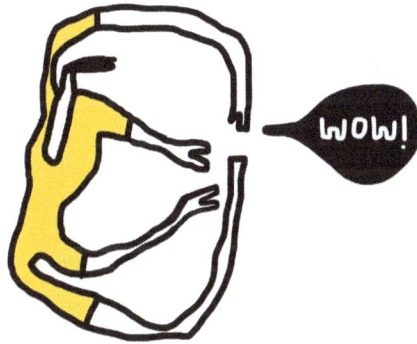

TO
COACHES, PRACTITIONERS
AND LEARNING DESIGNERS

When students assume a more active and autonomous role in their learning process, inevitably the traditional roles of teachers are also fundamentally transformed. Instead of lecturing and transmitting information accumulated from years of training in a particular field, the changing landscape of education professors will wear the different hats of coaches, facilitators, curators, practitioners and learning designers. Like their students, they must navigate new information from multiple sources and constantly update their knowledge, skills and educational resources. Of course their work and life experience matter and are employed to help steer students' self-determined learning journies by giving them procedural advice and tips on how to approach wicked problems; identify and use the information they need. Along the way, students also become teachers themselves for one another and the professor, sharing the content they generated, but also their best practices for a more effective learning experience:

> Teachers need to be very, very adaptive. They need to be able to change sociological professions three or four times a day: be a teacher, a journalist, a consultant, a director, all sorts of different things. We need to be able to adapt to different forms. [...] The system we are in makes teachers very secure. (Piotr Wołkow-iński, Lead Expert in URBACT, Poland)

Coaching is increasingly recognized as an important element in educational programs designed to promote CIE. It is a personalized, continuous and context-specific process during which the coach talks with the learners to better understand and monitor their progress through self-reflection. The coach asks students how their project is currently advancing, and explains the goals and the strategies chosen to meet these goals. Unlike life coaches, however, coaches in educational environments might also give advice on discipline-specific or content-related questions. Nevertheless, the emphasis during the coaching sessions is to enable learner-directed action and creative problem solving.[13] For this reason, coaches try to motivate learners by celebrating successes, but without withholding critical feedback that points to missed opportunities or harmful attitudes. Overall, coaching develops a supportive relationship between the student and the teacher but requires proper training and preparation. Careful observations during coaching sessions about the students' reflections on the trajectory of their projects and the course can be invaluable for curriculum design and content delivery:

> The biggest challenge is to shift the mindset of teachers who have been thought to teach, that's what they learnt, and now we are asking to think differently – take the backseats and let the students try and just guide them, to support them in their path to

find the answers that they need to find. (Vera Martinho, Senior Education Manager at Junior Achievement Europe)

Another important role for educators in the 21st-century learning landscape is that of a **curator**. The metaphor of educators as curators changes the established perceptions of curriculum development. Curation is the process of selecting, synthesizing and presenting content and different information. Traditionally, the content delivered in a course was independent from a teacher's personal interests and changed very little from year to year. On the contrary, curation implies a close connection to and concern about the materials collected. As Dean and Forray[14] point out, curation derives from the Latin verb *curare*, to care. Approaching curriculum development like an art or a museum exhibit permits the teacher to collect pieces that they personally value and care about, while allowing the students to wander on their own and make personal discoveries about their meaning. Educational curation forces educators to move beyond textbooks and a well-known set of materials and to experiment with new content and methodologies:

> *Practically there is no sense of basing entrepreneurship education on 20-years old cases from the USA on Kentucky Fried Chicken. The attention will rather be paid to the local and currently emerging cases, stimulating students to model possible solutions. If students in a class cannot imagine that the problem and the case to be real, it will look artificial to them.* (Prof. Agnis Stībe, Professor of Transformation in EM Normandie, France)

In the past it was considered largely undesirable or inappropriate for university professors to be active beyond their academic walls. Now, having experience and ongoing interactions with industry and society at large, ensuring that their work reaches the real world is becoming a must. Although oftentimes teaching and practicing is associated with workload pressures and professional burnouts, according to the "Teacher as Practitioner" project, "even small amounts of practitioner activity can increase the quality of the teaching."[15] The premise here is that by actively engaging with the local ecosystem, educators better learn about the context in which their students' projects will take place and share responsibility with other social stakeholders. As the demands for more meaningful collaborations between universities with industry, civil society and policy makers increase, teachers that are also practitioners will serve as connectors between the theory and the real-world practice, between the learners and experts, to provide immersive learning opportunities:

> *We have seen lots of businesses reaching out, offering mentoring and internships to students. It is definitely coming in a big way.* (Rachel Chan, The University of Hong Kong)

Finally, many educators, especially for CIE, are becoming **learning designers or use the help of learning designers to design better educational experiences.** Learning design is dedicated to creating, producing, evaluating, and improving resources and experiences that help people and organizations learn more and perform better. A learning design is a creative pathway, not driven by specific disciplines:

> *Teachers of the future don't necessarily come from the domain, but they have genuine capabilities in learning and learning design, and they leverage people with domain expertise such as academics or industry. Of course as well as teachers of future they have a toolkit of those skills, they can work across a range of different courses and programs, regardless of school or college.* (Dan Sleeman, Head of Design and Education, RMIT Activator)

A learning design consists of an amalgamation of several contemporary design traditions actively used within current teaching, learning, training and development professions.[16] Learning designers have opportunities to develop conditions, strategies, resources, tools and platforms that will keep learners engaged and inspired; help people make new connections and meanings, spark new interests and develop new abilities so that new learning will occur:

> *Everything starts with the teacher's empowerment.* (Sara Roversi, Future Food Institute, Italy)

> *We have internships, mentorships and job sharefrom businesses, but why can't we have the same for teachers - we want mentoring with business so we have something to say to the students.* (Teresa Franqueira, Director of Design Factory Aveiro, Portugal)

3 SUBJECT MATTER: FROM DISCIPLINARY-CENTERED TO MULTIDISCIPLINARY, PROBLEM- AND CHALLENGE-BASED LEARNING

FROM
DISCIPLINARY-CENTERED...

TO
MULTIDISCIPLINARY, PROBLEM AND CHALLENGE-BASED LEARNING

Education is traditionally organized by discipline. Our learning environments are driven by teachers, the content is separated into subjects and students choose between them according to their career expectations. Future-oriented learning needs a better connection between subjects and students where learning is closely related to real-world contexts and contemporary issues. HEIs globally need

> to think more holistically about the delivery of the value that it (university) provides over knowledge and the qualification. (Dan Sleeman, RMIT Activator, Head of Design and Education, Australia)

To extend learning into the real world, it must tackle challenges and problems associated with real contexts, organizations and societies such as the Sustainable Development Goals (SDGs). The SDGs were adopted by the United Nations in 2015 as a universal call to action to end poverty, protect the planet and ensure that by 2030 all people enjoy peace and prosperity. Education for Sustainable Development (ESD) is a key element of the 2030 Agenda for Sustainable Development. Its aims form one of the targets of the SDG on education SDG 4.7 and it is considered a driver for the achievements of all 17 SDGs.[17]

Generally, putting SDGs at the center of education practices requires an extension to the subject-centered view of education. It requires knowledge that spans different disciplines.[18] Prior academic work indicates that effective boundary-crossing innovation involves engaging with a diversity of other people and perspectives – not just other academics but also nonacademic stakeholders from private, public and civil sectors in interdisciplinary and transdisciplinary research processes.[19] Interdisciplinary challenge-based learning appears as a way to encourage students to work actively with peers, teachers and stakeholders in society to identify complex challenges, formulate relevant questions and take action.[20] Overall, there is a shift in the learning system to be more holistic and less siloed:

> But I can see the change already in my children and the ways they are being educated: it's very project-oriented, and they have to bring all digital skills, problem solving, system skills together. So the learning is way more holistic and less siloed. (Susann Roth, ADB, Philippines)

In some cases, traditional disciplines are less bound by a specific field of knowledge but are insead linked to certain themes and challenges that transcend established boundaries. For instance, in the case of the US-based school Minerva, the programs focus on the big questions:

> *So instead of doing something like the French Revolution, you do something like, how do we solve climate change, and that becomes your context through which you learn things like data analysis and manipulation, looking at climate change over time throughout history to see the empirical evidence behind something as large as climate change...embedding those big questions into the curriculum.* (Student, Minerva)

Dealing with these big questions often involves collaborating with external partners and bringing students to different geographical contexts following blended formats. Nesta (formerly NESTA, National Endowment for Science, Technology and the Arts), an innovation foundation based in the UK, frames them as challenge-driven university models where students draw on many disciplines to solve problems by working together and collaborating with organizations outside HEI.[21]

Shifts from subject-centered education allow us to question discipline boundaries and to emphasize the importance of interdisciplinarity:

> *One of the things we did is to be completely interdisciplinary, there are no subjects, there are no disciplines, everyone is connected to everything else, which is really important because reality is interdisciplinary. The workforce is increasingly interdisciplinary, and you need to be in order to be a creative innovator. So there are no subjects.* (Raya Bidshahri, Founder & CEO, School of Humanity, UAE)

This shift does not mean that disciplines become obsolete. Instead, they are becoming essential building blocks that learners bring to develop interdisciplinary collaboration and extend their own disciplines and/or solve problems by combining insights from different disciplines. For example, UCL ran a course for EdTech start up's called EDUCATE. The staff on this course came from many different faculties within the University:

> *They were training the students there to think across subjects about topics, rather than about subjects, making it as if there were no boundaries.* (Clare Stead, CEO, Oliiki, UK)

The most popular approaches to engage learners into SDGs are problem-based learning (PBL)[22] and challenge-based learning (CBL) activities.[23] The PBL is an instructional learner-centered approach that empowers learners to conduct research, integrate theory and practice and to apply knowledge and skills to develop a viable solution to a defined problem. The main difference between the two is that in PBL the problem is specific whereas CBL learners are presented with an open, relevant, problematic situation that requires a real solution. CBL is a learning experience where the learning takes place through the identification, analysis and design of a solution to a sociotechnical problem.

There are a few promising examples of challenge-driven initiatives that HEIs have put in place. Aalto University, a public research university located in Finland, for example, runs four interdisciplinary "factories" – design, health, media and service, where academics and students work with companies and communities to develop new products that respond to demand from the real economy. The Norwegian University of Science and Technology has "villages" (i.e., area of interest) of around 30 members who address questions such as "Biofuels – a solution or a problem?," "Sustainable, affordable housing for all" and "Portable technology and well-being." Each village is run by a professor who divides students into smaller groups to work on problems in their topic area.[24]

So far only a few HEIs have implemented CBLs strategically. Most of these programs appear at the departmental or individual level. The universities support these initiatives as add-on products but do not necessarily place them at the core of their curricula. Many others mostly collaborate with EdTech or education providers offering their services to traditional HEIs. For example, universities use challenges and crowd-based competitions to give the students possibilities for a broader range of experiences. iGEM, for example, is an annual competition run by the BioBricks foundation where university students design new products using synthetic biology. Agorize was created initially as a crowdsourcing platform for students. Aweacademy, an award-winning organization that teaches young minds skills, values and mindsets that are often not covered in traditional school curricula:

> And our long term mission is to create alternative models of schooling that would serve as a better fit for purpose to this world with accelerating change that we're living in. (Raya Bidshahri, Founder & CEO, School of Humanity, UAE)

Overall, we see that challenge- and problem-based learning are pioneering a new way to interdisciplinary education. Disciplines are still important and in-depth expertise in specific knowledge domains remains critical. However, discipline-specific knowledge is more valuable when it crosses scientific boundaries and when learners are encouraged to reflect on why they use certain disciplinary knowledge in the context of the problem/challenge that they currently work on. Focusing on specific themes and challenges give students a holistic understanding of different topics in context, helping them work across disciplines and transcend academic boundaries with blended learning:

> *We are not students of some subject matter, but students of problems. And problems may cut right across the boundaries of any discipline.* (Karl Popper, Conjectures and Refutations: The Growth of Scientific Knowledge)

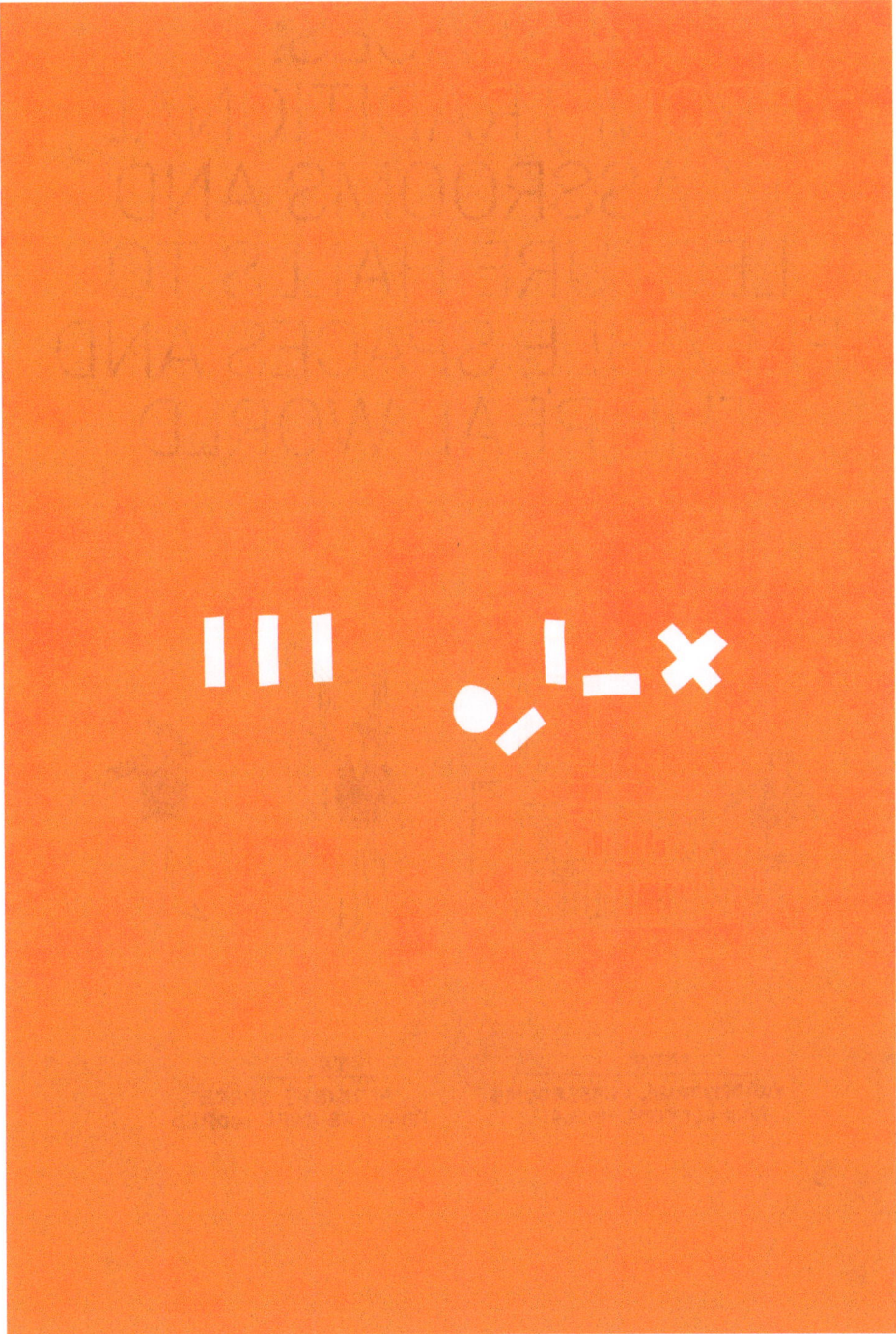

4 SPACES: FROM TRADITIONAL CLASSROOMS AND LECTURE HALLS TO FLEXIBLE SPACES AND THE REAL WORLD

FROM
TRADITIONAL CLASSROOMS
AND LECTURE HALLS...

TO
FLEXIBLE SPACE
AND THE REAL WORLD

A defining feature of modern education is the classroom or lecture hall with rows of chairs facing forward toward a board or screen. School and university spaces have been modeled on the lecture paradigm of learning, whereby knowledge is transmitted by an instructor through a presentation on a specific topic. Architecturally, learning spaces have been designed for lectures, as well as keeping knowledge accessible only to those in the classroom and more broadly, tightly contained within institutional walls, separated from the real world.

Over the past couple of decades, lecture-based education and the boundaries between academia and society have been challenged, and this has brought into question current infrastructure and facilities for learning. As is emphasized in other sections of this publication, challenge-driven and experiential learning requires students to work together in teams and engage with their professors not as lecturers but as coaches and mentors. Furthermore, and especially when it comes to CIE, learners need to meaningfully interact with the world outside of academic walls to better understand the challenge of innovating and ensuring that their solutions are effective and relevant. It is important, therefore, to consider the physical environment in which learning takes place.

There is a rich literature on the importance of space for innovation and building communities.[25] It is only recently that attention has been put on the spaces for learning beyond traditional classrooms. An alternative to the rigid and literally fixed structure of big lecture halls are "flexible spaces."[26] These spaces are designed to accommodate different furniture and layout options, which in turn enable a variety of learning styles. For example, in these flexible spaces, chairs and desks can be positioned in rows for lectures, but also arranged in groups to create space for teamwork or separated completely to allow coworking outside the regular classroom hours. Shared workspaces for facilitate collaboration and allow more focused work on ideas, community creation and promote a general ambiance of well-being.[27]

A study conducted with students at RMIT University in Melbourne looked closely at how the design of educational facilities impacts how students learn.[28] Unsurprisingly, the study indicated that there is a mismatch between the kinds of spaces students find useful and desirable and the existing lecture or tutorial rooms. Furthermore, students reported that they liked being in flexible spaces of learning that accommodate both individual and collaborative work. Case studies of flexible learning environments in secondary education[29] show evidence that these new learning spaces "facilitate student-centered pedagogy and self-regulation, collaboration, and student autonomy and engagement,"[30] in addition to being more enjoyable and comfortable for the students. These flexible learning spaces don't only have to be physical. Indeed, hit by COVID-19, we saw how rapidly classes were delivered online. Technology can assist by providing a blended learning environment where teachers can post resources and assignments that allow students a degree of control over their own learning path, pace, time and even place. Immersive learning spaces that combine physical and digital spaces and blend them in a creative way will be increasingly used in the future. Immersive learning places put individuals in an interactive learning environment, either physically or virtually, to replicate possible scenarios or to teach particular skills or techniques. Simulations, role play and virtual learning environments can be considered immersive learning.

For example, the University of Sydney has one of the largest immersive learning labs used for teaching where students have access to the immersive content based on interactive 360° videos of real environments or constructed virtual realities. One of the experiences is centered on humanitarian engineering where students explore villages in Niger to learn how to apply their core engineering skills to complex humanitarian problems.

Taking students from the traditional classroom[31] into a learning environment built for teamwork and challenge-driven innovation that requires interaction with the real world requires new methodologies and techniques. Design thinking[32] and ethnographic methods[33] offer many concrete elements that have been recorded in the innovation literature. Below, we present a related but less well-known methodology for guiding learners, *literally*, out from the brick-and-mortar walls of education institutions into the streets and wilds. This methodology finds its roots in Ancient Greece's "peripatetic school" linked to Aristotle.

The name of the school itself, *peripatetic*, reveals the methodology we would like to emphasize here. *Peripatikos* is an adjective that means "of walking" and Aristotle's students were called *peripatetikoi* in reference to their habit of walking while teaching and learning. As ably reported by the TACIT Knowledge Alliance Project[34] "deep or long-term learning occurs when individuals are taken outside of the context of application and where experiential and compelling stories link the landscape and the learner to create knowledge scaffolds." In a nutshell, peripatetic learning can happen through visiting and exploring different kinds of locations, from industrial heritage sites to rural areas. One task of the learners in this journey is to develop innovation scenarios and creative solutions using their experiences and locations they observe.

> *If you can design the physical space, the social space, and the information space together to enhance collaborative learning, then that whole milieu turns into a learning technology.* (John Seely Brown)

LEARNING JOURNEY

Learning journey captures how the knowledge is structured and transmitted to individuals. Learning journey denotes the way we learn including styles of learning and processes of learning on the one side and physical material and digital technologies on the other. Physical materials and digital technologies can be seen as enablers for effective learning journeys. Through learning style and processes, learning journeys foster new forms of education. These forms are learner-centric in that they allow people to learn with the support of the physical materials that are most conducive to their progress: post-its, sketches, prototypes, Lego bricks, etc.

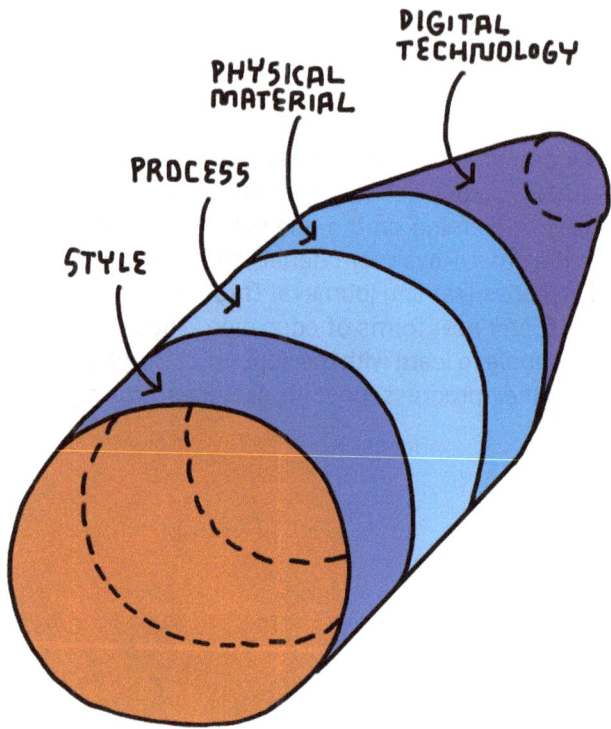

STYLE

PROCESS

PHYSICAL
MATERIAL

DIGITAL
TECHNOLOGY

PART I

5 Style: From individual and independent to team-based and collaborative learning

Learning style must take individual preferences and passions into account. Education systems need to better recognize that each individual learns differently and the systems need to move from didactic learning practices to collaborative learning where individual preferences are recognized and considered. Learning styles need to balance between individualistic and collectivistic preferences for learning and carefully design learning journeys by integrating these styles in a balanced and flexible way.

6 Process: From linear to iterative, exploratory and experimental

Didactic approaches to teaching where the teacher selects the topic, controls the content and receives a response in a linear way do little to build the depth of thinking and iterative exploration needed for a life-like experience. There is a shift toward more iterative, exploratory and experimental learning processes where play, experimentation and exploration are supported. A shift is needed to help learners iterate and balance between the objective and subjective, the practical and the theoretical, and the imaginative and the critical throughout their learning.

7 Physical material: From blackboards and textbooks to arts and crafts

Learning by doing in flexible environments is crucial, and play and playfulness demonstrate their importance in adult learning. Consequently, a new set of physical learning materials is increasingly being used in classrooms to facilitate teamwork, communication and experimentation. Many tools and techniques are available to make learning more interactive and engaging – sketches, post-its, prototypes and serious games (to name a few) demonstrate their relevance for facilitating the play and exploration needed for CIE.

8 Digital technologies: From one-directional to interactive uses

Technology has become part of everything that we do. Education is not an exception. In a world that relies on technology, analog and one-directional learning practices cannot prepare learners for what they will face as adults, or make them future ready. HEIs need to move from one-directional use of technologies to interactive uses that allow users to bridge learning within the university and connect it to the outside world.

5 STYLE: FROM INDIVIDUAL AND INDEPENDENT TO TEAM-BASED AND COLLABORATIVE LEARNING

FROM
INDIVIDUAL
AND INDEPENDENT...

TO
TEAM-BASED
AND COLLABORATIVE

In the past, even if education happened in groups, the same content was delivered to all students in the same way and students were expected to learn individually and independently. We are aware that education systems need to better recognize that individuals learn differently, and their preferences also change over time. In fact, education that focuses on creating the best possible learning experience drives the future of learning. Learning should be brought back to the learners to account for their preferences individually and in the group. Designing experiences that reflect the learning styles and preferences of each learner is crucial. RMIT School of Education Professor, Tricia McLaughlin, indicated "Experiences that allow collaboration, communication, and teamwork for all students often happen beyond classroom walls. We need to facilitate for these experiences in context, and our classrooms need to be a reflection of this."[35]

Learners are often conceptualized as active and engaged participants. Learner participation is central, where "learning by doing" is a founding concept.[36] It is a "hands-on" task-oriented process, which is based on direct experience[37] where learners are proactive in their education and collaborate with their peers. As the Head of Education at RMIT Activator, Dan Sleeman, pointed out:

> our focus mostly is on the development of capabilities and the facilitation of creative thinking in collaboration. Because we believe that growth is paramount for people's development.

He also emphasized that

> we condition students as today's recipients of information rather than contributors to information exchange and so where we're trying to kind of break away from that idea of didactic learning and thinking more about how we learn through collaborative experience.

Collaborative experience requires teamwork and collaborative learning: spaces are designed to emphasize collaboration between students (see chapter on Spaces); openness and flexibility of the curricula. Collaborative learning is defined as a teaching approach that involves learners working in pairs or small groups to discuss concepts and find solutions to problems. In collaborative learning, students need to work toward a common goal. They should develop a sense of accountability among themselves and self-manage collaboration. The goal is to enhance critical thinking, communication skills and to foster responsibility. Collaborative learning does not imply only learning in groups: it is a combination of learning individually, in pairs and in teams while reflecting one's own preferences for learning. The collaboration itself is not only among students but also includes teachers and other stakeholders (e.g., industry, government, start-ups, hospitals) to help students gain a variety of different perspectives.

To ensure effective collaboration experience, design-driven practices are used more and more in the classroom to facilitate collaborative learning experience:

> *Design is about creating ways to bring people together, who may not be used to the idea, into a rich, collaborative environment.* (Stefan Jakobek, education lead at HOK)

As Almajed and colleagues indicated: "The idea is to put disparate people together in one place, so maybe if a person studying Ebola bumps into someone focused on the human genome, they might have this great conversation and new ideas are sparked."[38]

Learning is a social activity. Still, when thinking about collaborative learning, we need to carefully acknowledge different learning styles, and perhaps combine different learning activities:

> *What it did was to change the route dynamics in the classroom. So the quiet kids would, you know, be given the space to take the lead. And the loud kids would realize they learned something from the quiet kids as well.* (Raya Bidshahri, Founder & CEO, School of Humanity, UAE)

EdTech companies are experimenting with spaces for *personalized learning pathways, to cater to different preferences.* To be able to integrate these preferences, many turn to neuroscience and neuroeducation:

> *So a lot of schools are taking this scientific approach, for example, having two classes, two different types of activities for the same content, and then measure which group does better... there is an increasing number of neuroscientists that are speaking to educators and creating that link between how we understand the brain learns best and then mirroring our school systems around that. So that's a huge area that I think will inform best practices in the future.* (Raya Bidshahri, Founder & CEO, School of Humanity, UAE)

PART I

There is a need to combine both collective and individualistic practices to learning:

> *So you need both, you need the personal drive of the self-direct-*
> *ed, lifelong learning individual, while it's being held by peers in the*
> *collective so you have one foot in the individualistic and one foot*
> *in the collectivistic world of learning.* (Sandra Otto, co-founder
> of Future of Work Collective)

Collaborative learning does not just occur within one discipline. HEIs around the world are creating spaces for interdisciplinary learning that are necessary for tackling complex problems (see Subject Matter and Spaces). CIE learning is interdisciplinary:

> *It's also responsive to students, and their interest in locating and*
> *bringing creativity to a broad spectrum of situations. I was teach-*
> *ing technology so you know, I often would also collaborate with our*
> *computer scientist, cross-disciplinary projects.* (Vice President of
> Academic Affairs for Minneapolis College of Art and Design)

As prior research indicates, creative potential is enhanced by the diversity of different groups.[39] Yet, at the same time diverse groups can lead to potential conflicts, absence of cohesion and information sharing. "Perspective taking" is emphasized to help individuals creatively manage their interactions.[40] Despite the benefits of collaborative learning, training for collaborative problem solving is still scarce.[41] Paul Gardiner conducted a review of different practices for collaborative learning and developed a framework scaffold for collaborative thinking in educational contexts to help students generate creative responses to complex problems.[42] This framework for epistemic control focuses on developing students' metacognitive understanding and epistemic awareness to enable meaningful epistemic shifting, perspective taking and cross disciplinary communication. Moving from epistemic awareness, through epistemic humility and epistemic empathy, students develop epistemic control.[43] When designing collaborative learning experiences in interdisciplinary settings, we need to reflect upon the epistemic position within learning practices to ensure inclusive collaboration and to support creativity.

Finally, with an increasing shift to online and blended learning, we need to design optimal technology-supported collaborative learning (see Digital Technologies). Given the focus on people working together, there are complex and dynamic interactions that may, or may not, be easily identifiable by computers (e.g., body language, cultural differences, emotions, linguistic styles).[44] Technology used for collaboration needs to include (1) a joint task, (2) communication, (3) sharing of resources, (4) engagement in productive processes, (5) engagement in co-construction, (6) monitoring and regulation and (7) finding and building groups and communities.[45]

Collaboration is at the center of CIE learning practice and CIE is also an enabler for collaborative learning styles. Overall, cross-disciplinary learning practices give students the opportunity to view complex subjects through many different lenses, helping them to understand that one problem could relate to another and to learn how to deal with real-life problems.

> *When three people work together, each can be the teacher in some aspects.* (Confucius)

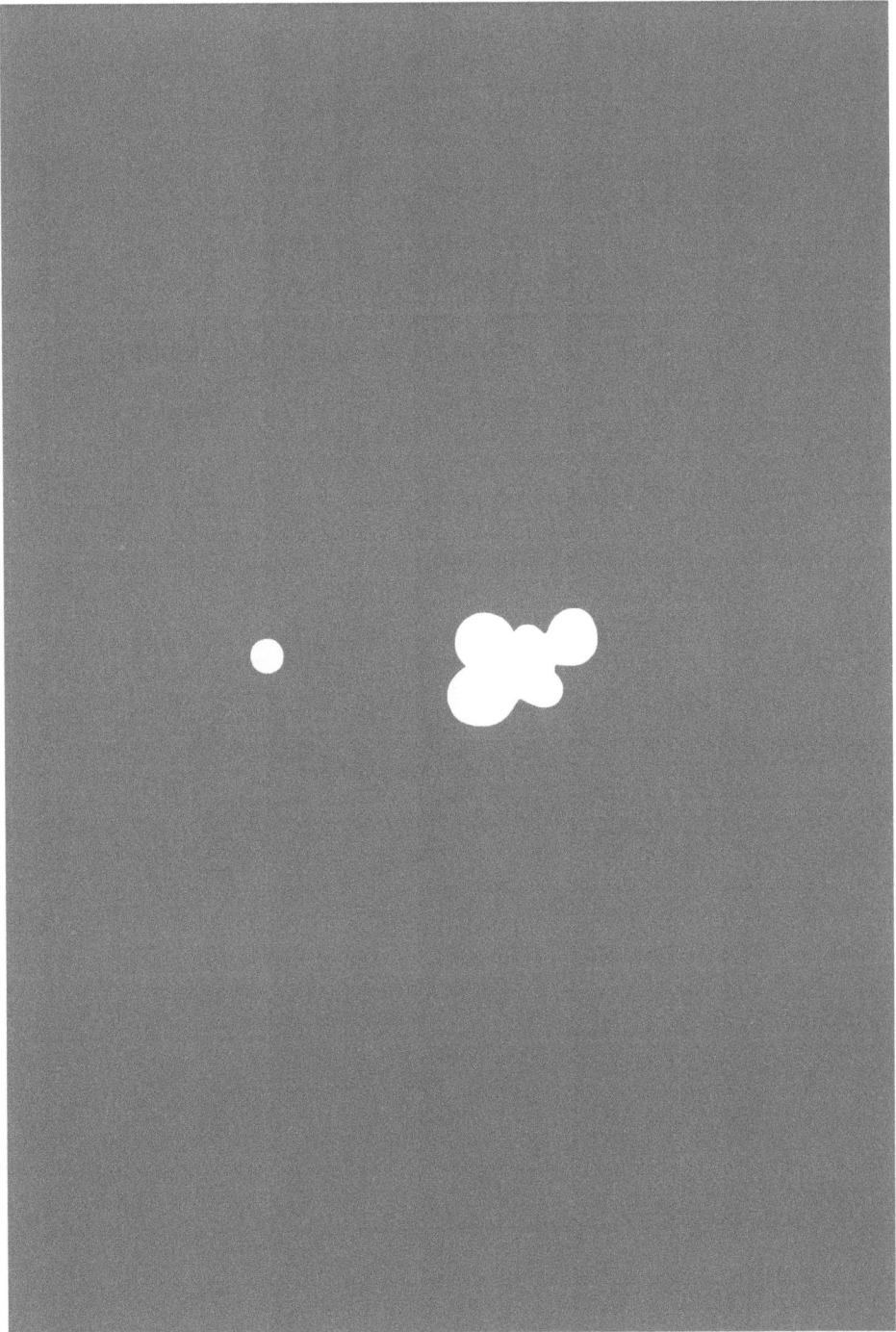

6 PROCESS: FROM LINEAR TO ITERATIVE, EXPLORATORY AND EXPERIMENTAL

FROM
LINEAR ...

TO
ITERATIVE, EXPLORATORY
AND EXPERIMENTAL

Education systems should empower learners to develop skills and competencies to cope with a constantly changing landscape. To achieve this, new types of pedagogies are required to help our education system shift from linear to iterative learning journeys that facilitate play, experimentation and exploration. To be future-ready, learners need to be able to iterate and balance the objective and subjective, the practical and the theoretical, and the imaginative and the critical throughout their learning. It is important to avoid the artificial divide and ensure a holistic learning experience.

"Learning journey" is defined as a learning experience that occurs over a period and involves a series of different learning elements and learning experiences involving different methods and channels. Learning journeys and processes are becoming more flexible and adjusted to the needs of lifelong learners. Learners can choose specific predefined routes or follow different approaches to their learning by building their skills through a combination of different courses in different institutions. As pointed out in the article by Future Learn: "Differentiated learning will provide each learner with the opportunities to move their learning forward on many fronts and to reach different points on the horizon."[46] This represents lifelong learning and helps learning to create a sense of agency:

> *What we are really doing - we are just facilitating your learning journey and we're doing that by providing a bunch of different support mechanisms. It could be coaching and mentorship and some learning resources. You know, like learning design where every week we have a weekly stand up with all the teams. There's not much of a traditional curriculum. There's no real assessment, but what we get out of that as a result, as we get humans that have complete agency over their learning journey, driven to achieve a particular result because it's really attached to something they care deeply about.* (Dan Sleeman, Head of Design and Education, RMIT Activator)

What we see is that the learning journey should be designed as a fluid, holistic, seamless set of experiences (see Students for more information on personalized learning). To further emphasize the role of experience, experiential learning theory (ELT) can be used. ELT provides a holistic model of the learning process and a multilinear model of adult development, both of which are consistent with what we know about how people learn, grow and develop.[47] The theory is called experiential learning to emphasize the central role that experience plays in the learning process, an emphasis that distinguishes ELT from other learning theories.[48] Derived from social constructivism, ELT emphasizes "learning by doing" and is described as the "process whereby knowledge is created through the transformation of experience."[49] Almost 2,400 years ago Aristotle wrote: "for the things we have to learn before we can do them, we learn by doing them." John Dewey indicated: "give the pupils something to do, not something to learn; and the doing is of such a nature as to demand thinking; learning naturally results."

For example, Minneapolis College of Art and Design (MCAD) is based on John Dewey's ideas of experiential learning and it was founded as a place for adults to teach adults. As the Vice President of Academic Affairs of MCAD indicated:

> The notion of adult education was born there. And, you know, you as an engineer could come into the new school and perhaps share for the first time in your life, your deep love and knowledge of Shakespeare, or something else like engineering itself, or mathematics or whatever could be combined.

One of MCAD values is experiential learning. It embraces generative processes, critical discourse, and an iterative methodology to help learners achieve academic, institutional and individual excellence (for more information on this case, refer to Part II).

During the process of doing and making things, students experiment and learn in the process. They learn by doing. In one of the interviews, Sandra Otto, Co-founder of Future Work Collectives in New Zealand pointed out:

> So the key element for learning for me is learning by doing. So basically, there's our secret: there's absolute minimal theory, like I might say, here's a lifelong learning matrix (interest and mastery in the axes), I draw it on a white-board and say, Go take a piece of paper, and now you do it, apply it to your own real life. (Sandra Otto, co-founder of Future of Work Collective)

As described above, the learning process is becoming iterative, exploratory and experimental for all students involved. There is a general acknowledgment of the importance of play and experiments in lifelong learning. Curriculum design should incorporate these practices carefully,

> we could keep designing classes and integrate more learning experiences to fill probably 10 year's worth of a degree. But that's not real. It's not realistic. So how do we step back and think about what are, you know, kind of foundational experiences and knowledge sets that allow one to then continue to learn throughout life? (Robert Ransick, Vice President of Academic Affairs, MCAD)

Different methods and approaches can help students embrace iterative and experiential learning practices. For example, anticipation-action-reflection (AAR) is an iterative learning process whereby learners continuously improve their thinking and act intentionally and responsibly toward collective well-being. Different programs use tools such as design thinking, concept-knowledge driven processes, agile tools and SCRUM to engage learners in a process of iterative learning, often through problem solving and testing.

Iterative design and learning comes from the world of programming, in which cyclic processes of prototyping, testing, analyzing, and refining a product or process are common. For instance, in the Incremental Build Model, code is developed one portion at a time, with heavy testing and input along the way. Behind such approaches, lurks the sea-change that is the Agile Movement, in which requirements and solutions evolve from collaboration between self-organizing, cross-functional teams through evolutionary development, early delivery and continuous improvement. Considering the rapidly changing, collaborative environment we work in these days, it is easy to see why an "agile" mindset, manifested by iterative design, is increasingly essential to meet the demands of learners and their institutions. For example, Design thinking is an iterative process that provides a solution-based approach to solving problems. Using a structured framework, students identify challenges, gather information, generate potential solutions, refine ideas and test solutions. Throughout this iterative process students are encouraged to understand the user, challenge assumptions and redefine problems. Recent works have emphasized the need for students to learn to combine divergent and convergent thinking in a collaborative, controlled manner.[50] Embedding elements of concept–knowledge (C-K) theory can help to manage bottlenecks, challenges that students encounter in exploration and help to clarify and overcome them by providing means of action. By combining different approaches and tools, educators and trainers can design the learning experiences adapted to each learning journey and track its progress.

While embedding shifts to more iterative learning and experimentation, we need to account for different learning preferences and to create a safe environment:

> *The key to any successful learning journey is psychological safety and trust* (Sandra Otto, co-founder of Future of Work Collective)

Different tools can be used to create a sense of safe space as well:

> *And the key tool that we use is what we call the Authentic Check-in. In a four hour lab, or an innovation sprint, I might spend one hour out of the four hours on the Authentic Check-in, which sounds like a massive amount of time. But the productivity creativity and transformational capacity afterwards is astounding. It's so powerful because the egos go out of the room, which can be a huge issue in corporations.* (Sandra Otto, co-founder of Future of Work Collective)

Making learning processes iterative and experimental requires changes not only in the way we teach and organize the content but also in how we embed more reflective and interactive ways to evaluate learning results (see Learning Results). This is an important shift and requires redressing an imbalance in teaching to facilitate a more real-world experience for the benefit of students:

> *It is amazing how dispiriting it can be to enter a learning environment and to be made immediately to suppress your own exploratory inclinations. So many learning environments in the world are still like this...We owe it to ourselves and each other to create better opportunities that enhance human potential.* (Ashim Shanker, Sinew of the Social Species)

7 PHYSICAL MATERIAL: FROM BLACKBOARDS AND TEXTBOOKS TO ARTS AND CRAFTS

FROM BLACKBOARDS AND TEXTBOOKS...

TO ARTS AND CRAFT

In a traditional classroom one is expected to find a blackboard or whiteboard for teachers to guide instruction. One might also expect to find textbooks or note-books for students to follow and review the content presented. The physical material required for didactic lecture-based learning is simple and straightforward. On the contrary, CIE learning environments often resemble arts and crafts workshops with a whole new set of creative materials to be used for learning purposes.

As explained in the previous sections on the shifts in the spaces and styles of learning, CIE demands a more interactive and collaborative engagement of students whereby "learning by doing" in flexible environments plays an important role. Consequently, a new set of physical learning materials is increasingly being used in classrooms to facilitate teamwork, communication, and experimentation. These include sticky notes, colored papers, pens and markers, cardboard, stickers, tape and Legos.[51]

Sticky notes or post-its, are particularly popular in CIE learning environments. In the article "Post-it note pedagogy"[52] the author suggests that these colorful pieces of sticky paper are a creative, engaging and flexible means to engage students in the classroom. Because they come with a relatively small space for writing, they encourage students to synthesize and be concise with their thoughts and ideas. Most importantly they can be used in learning in CIE in a variety of ways, and particularly for ideation.

For example, students are asked to write down their ideas and thoughts on a specific topic on different sets of sticky notes. Then the instructor or the students themselves can begin grouping these together to identify collective areas of interest. There are many ways ideas can be reorganized to prioritize and generate meaning, from "the ideas tree" to "diamond nine models" and "pyramid of priorities."

Another well-known set of materials used for teaching innovation are spaghetti sticks and marshmallows for the so-called marshmallow challenge. This is a competition-like exercise with the goal to build the tallest structure with the materials provided. Students work in teams and therefore must negotiate a set of different ideas and designs. In the process, a set of assumptions are challenged (e.g., the marshmallows are not as light as we might have first imagined) and the importance of teamwork and prototyping is highlighted as critical elements that drive innovation.

Prototyping is of course a critical element for learning CIE and one where arts and crafts materials are needed, especially during the earlier stages of the innovation journey where students iterate many versions of their ideas before reaching their final design and product. Known as "low-fidelity prototyping," these models are created to visualize and make an idea tangible, so that they can better communicate and test it among the team or users. They are usually simple and incomplete and are made from cheap materials such as cardboard, wooden sticks, cloth and ribbons.

Some of the simplest examples of low-fidelity prototypes are sketches and diagrams and paper interfaces. The latter are particularly useful for illustrating how a new app might work. Using similar principles as the first animations, multiple sheets of paper are used with movable elements and interactive features that can illustrate how a user would interface with the proposed product.[53]

Lego is another physical tool that has gradually entered CIE learning spaces over the past two decades and is currently employed in many ways to enhance innovation. Because of its three-dimensional modular design, Lego pieces are used to craft landscape models that can better communicate ideas or the user experience. The LEGO® SERIOUS PLAY® methodology builds on research that demonstrates that hands-on learning generates deeper insights about the topic at hand. It also draws on Plato's observation that "you can learn about a person in an hour of play than you can from a lifetime of conversation."[54] In a nutshell, using selected Lego elements, participants are asked to build their own models first in response to a specific question or challenge. These models subsequently serve to stimulate discussion and group problem solving.

Bringing the physical materials that over the past century have been confined to kindergarten and arts and crafts workshops into higher- or adult education opens possibilities for learning. It has been proven that arts and creative play triggers children's imagination and it is only natural that these become staple elements of all learning environments across different age groups and kinds of learners.[55] When it comes to adults, play and playfulness are manifested in the classroom through risk taking, storytelling and physical activities.[56]

An interesting example of this shift is the Bauhaus. The Bauhaus School operated in Germany between 1919 and 1933. As a school of thought, it advocated for a new way of approaching problems in art, architecture and design; and as a physical school in Weimar and Dessau it hosted a succession of prominent course leaders. Teachers included avant-garde artists like Johannes Itten, Paul Klee and Vassily Kandinsky, while Bauhaus students included Josef Albers, Herbert Bayer and Gunta Stölzl.[57]

As indicated on the Bauhaus website: "Education at the Bauhaus School was diverse and hands-on, spanning building theory, carpentry, ceramics, fine art, graphic printing, glass and mural painting, weaving, geometry, mathematics, business administration, metal, photography, printing and advertising and plastic arts. Even parties and stage performances were part of the curriculum, with students encouraged to

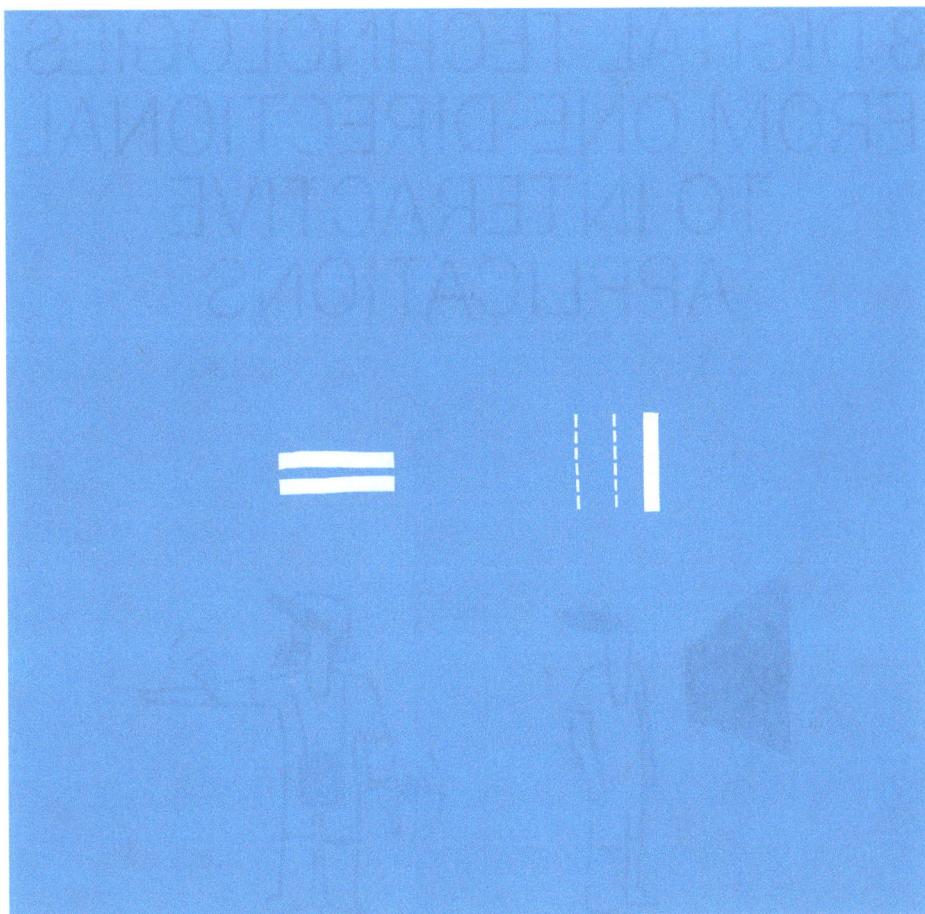

experiment in costume and stagecraft." The whole idea of a Bauhaus workshop – halfway between learning and production, between work and play, has become omnipresent in current education. The workshop, a format that encourages the application of what is learned in real time, permits teaching to adapt to what people need.[58]

There is a New European Bauhaus project that calls to collect experiences about beautiful, sustainable and inclusive forms of living. The project aims to co-design future ways of living, situated at the crossroads between art, culture, social inclusion, science and technology.[59]

> *The highest form of research is essentially play.* (N. V. Scarfe, education researcher)

8 DIGITAL TECHNOLOGIES: FROM ONE-DIRECTIONAL TO INTERACTIVE APPLICATIONS

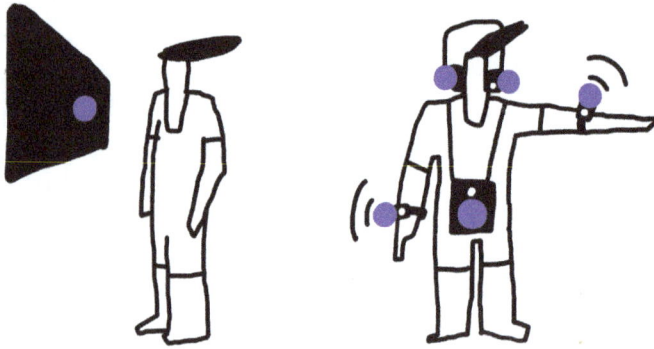

FROM
ONE-DIRECTIONAL ...

TO
INTERACTIVE APPLICATIONS

Traditionally schools were not isolated from technology, but technology was often limited to supporting existing practices and ways of teaching. Indeed, students have mostly learned how to use technology outside of the education system. Now, universities need to leverage technologies to liberate learning from outdated practices and allow learners to connect in a meaningful way that allows them to connect learning within the university to the outside world. We also believe that the educational institutions should prepare learning to navigate the increasing complexity of all digital and help dealing with the negative consequences of digital use (e.g., information overload, screen fatigue)

Advances in information and communication technologies (ICT), especially digital solutions, are revolutionizing the education sector. Technology is not just a support for education but is present in all elements of learning and teaching: course design and delivery, outcome measurement and tracking learning progress. As Santoso Garcia has pointed out, technology is one of the main drivers of skills obsolescence and skills mismatch leading to numerous Implications for the labor market, society and the economy.[60] At the same time, technology is a powerful driver of human development. The relationship between technology and society can best be described as a synergistic cycle of codependency, co-influence and co-production, leading to paradoxical situations.[61] As we see, 4th industrial revolution, digital transformation and exponential technology growth create growing pressure on individuals to constantly "update" themselves, organizations to ensure that their human resource management (HRM) is adaptable to changing business needs and for universities to shift their curricula to adjust to the emerging needs.

As an example, let's look at the use of AI to create personalized and context-specific learning where students can access the content anywhere and anytime can foster CIE. For example, AI-based solutions can help create conversational chatbots for use in education with many potential benefits. Dr. Matthias Kaiser-swerth, managing director of Bern-based Hasler Foundation that supports several digitization initiatives in Switzerland, argued:

> *A chatbot doesn't tire, unlike a human. You can ask it the most stupid questions and it will still remain calm and give you an answer. It can nudge you and challenge you with questions that you will answer. And so it becomes basically a teacher that you could have available 24x7. Since the AI tool also doesn't judge a person, it could also reduce the hesitation/embarrassment of learners in asking questions that are perceived as being 'not intelligent.*

There is expectation that AI will help us to challenge the students to think differently about the material that they're reading:

> And it's not the critical thinking so much as the practice. It is the nature of the students getting that the artificial intelligence can pick up to help introduce students different concepts and help growth of their knowledge. (Paul Feldman, Chief Executive, JISC, UK)

The most dominant form of using technology in education is online modules and Massive Online Courses (MOOCs). The COVID-19 pandemic has pushed the use of MOOCs and the need for traditional universities to transfer existing offline courses into virtual formats. But what should be delivered online and how do we blend online and face-to-face learning effectively? We can see examples of universities that deliver lectures on theories and background knowledge online – making specific online degrees a prerequisite to enter a certain module or course. The time being present in the class can then be used in a much more efficient way; to interact with peers and try different things "hands-on." This form of collaboration between face-to-face and online forms of learning can enable working in smaller teams, involving industry, and learning in co-working spaces rather than large lecture halls.

Despite this potential, technology in the education sector is often, or even mostly, used to streamline and modernize existing practices. This is especially true for schools where foundations for future skills are laid. In the words of Tracy Burns, an education expert at the OECD:

> If you're looking at early childhood education and care, there's very little presence of technology, and what is there is often quite traditional. Despite the fact that it's in a way a brand new slate.

According to Tracy Burns, technology is not necessarily radically disrupting or changing practice or teaching. Rather, "it's more being used to sort of streamline and modernize what's already being done." One reason for this under-utilization of technology's potential seems to lie in the lack of familiarity that teaching staff have with modern technologies. Matthias Kaiserswerth, says that

> most teachers you find in schools have no clue about computer science and now they're sort of tasked with teaching it at least a few modules.

Technology's role in the future of learning will increase. We need to design efficient ways for machines and humans to create and exploit synergies between the technologies on the one hand and the unique and irreplaceable human (cognitive) capabilities, on the other. Closely related to this is the question of how to explore new ways for machines and humans to collaborate. Even though we have a much better understanding of where the niches for technology are and where the niches for human capabilities are, there is a lack of understanding about the potential impact of their interplay in terms of CIE. According to Börsch-Supan,

> *we talk fairly little about how machines and humans can fruitful-ly connect because I think there's a lot of fear in society that we will be replaced. Or that machines, in a way, are more intelligent than us. And I don't think that's true. I think they are about as intelligent as we make them. And there are surprisingly many things they can't do.*

It is, therefore, critical that learners and teachers not only engage in exploring the application part of technology but also develop a thorough understanding of its fundamentals. We need to explore the optimal trade-offs of using technologies to deliver better learning experiences.

However, fear of technology can be also found in the education sector, both with teachers and with students/learners. While students worry about their data safety and privacy, teachers may either not be sufficiently well-versed with the rapidly evolving technologies or might sometimes also feel threaten by technology. In some cases, they might also have apprehensions that the transmission of knowl-edge would not work as effectively and efficiently.

Blended learning with its emphasis on human/machine interaction can possibly make a useful contribution in improving our learning practices. The increasing success of blended learning formats shows that the handicaps of a purely technol-ogy-driven approach can be overcome with a well-orchestrated human-machine combination. However, to achieve the full potential of blended learning through ef-fective and productive human/technology interaction it is necessary that learning management systems and technology supports the *actual needs* of the learner.

Luise Degen, a research fellow at the Hamburg University of Technology, who spe-cializes in research on blended learning, cautions against a confusing plethora of technologies and tools. There are, in her opinion, so many different and fea-ture-rich tools used in blended learning "that one could be forgiven for believing that the fancier a technology is, the better it is." In her words,

> *what I'm going right now is the University Innovation Fellows Program and they're working with Wiki and with Moodle and with Zoom and with Google Drive and they are using so many different platforms that you can easily get overwhelmed and confused, especially because they all work very differently. And I think, having that in sync, for example through synchronous learning formats, can enhance the learning experience.*[62]

This points toward the need for more standardization, for example, in terms of technical interfaces, ease of use and accessibility of learning platforms.

Overall, the current use of technology in learning is not yet geared for the full realization of the possibilities of emerging and existing technologies, because their disruptive potential has been underutilized and existing practices have been streamlined. For promoting CIE, it is critical that this untapped potential is fully exploited, for example, by enabling learners and teachers through concerted measures to go beyond the mere application of technologies by developing a fuller understanding of technologies and how they work. This also necessitates processes of standardization, especially in the form of interfaces between different technologies and tools. When designing for a blended learning environment and introducing emerging technologies into a classroom, we need to be as inclusive as possible.

As a student from Minerva who we interviewed pointed out,

> *I think there's always some of the voices of the ones that are less wealthy, have lower social safety nets, I think, as almost always the loudest voices are the ones with money and the ones in power. And so yeah, I mean, more voices from people who don't have physical or tech literacy access need to be included.*

Overall, technology helps increase learning potential in the classroom and prepare students for their technological future. But, we need to be careful when introducing technology in the learning practices to avoid bad teaching experiences online and further increase inequality when it comes to technology literacy and simple access to technology:

> *Teachers need to integrate technology seamlessly into the curriculum instead of viewing it as an add-on, an afterthought, or an event.* (Heidi-Hayes Jacobs)

LEARNING RESULTS

What is it that you desire to achieve at the end of the learning journey? What would you like your students to know and be able to do at the end of course? What do they have to deliver and how will you evaluate their deliverables? What is the overall success of your program? In traditional education environments these questions are not very complicated to answer, but in environments that focus on creativity, innovation and entrepreneurship the learning outputs and outcomes, as well as their impact and evaluation, are not easily quantifiable. In this section, we focus on some important developments and current trends.

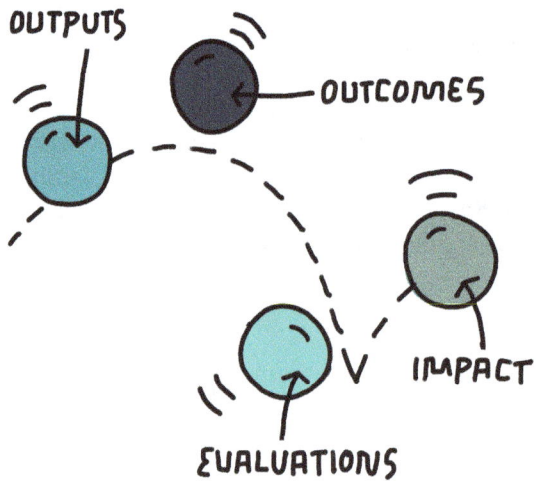

9 Outputs: From writing to doing and making

This shift captures an increasing need to not only understand our world and learn about it but to try to do something about it. This requires thinking about different learning outputs in CIE that include prototypes, real objects and sketches. In this chapter, we build on makerspaces, Fab Labs and DIY laboratories as forms of learning by doing that allow the creation of learning outputs connected to the real world.

10 Outcomes: From standardized knowledge acquisition to personalized knowledge, skills and attitudes

Learning should not only aim to provide job-ready skills but instead should help with future upskilling and reskilling. The focus is in developing transformative competencies that span the process of learning.

11 Impact: From institutional to societal

There is increasing pressure for education institutions to demonstrate their impact in research and teaching. The reflections on impact should include the impact of learning as well, focusing on preparing learners to deal with the societal challenges.

12 Evaluation: From one-dimensional to multidimensional

Effective evaluation of learning when the entire system of education is undergoing transformation is a challenging task. As learning outputs shift, evaluation needs to shift as well to the multidimensional aspects that reflect physical artifacts, competence- and skill-based outcomes and societal impact. Evaluation needs to carefully consider the collaborative and self-determined nature of learning, as well as the learning journey itself.

9 LEARNING OUTPUTS: FROM WRITING TO MAKING AND DOING

FROM
WRITING...

TO
TO MAKING AND DOING

There are two important points to consider in the shift toward "making" that this chapter focuses on. The first one concerns the growing demands across different disciplines for greater impact and relevance, which we address in the first two chapters of this book. More specifically, critics from both inside and outside academia have raised doubts about the rational-analytic emphasis in teaching and research rather than attention to the practical and messier day-to-day challenges experienced in the real world.[63] Grasping different phenomena is not enough if these learnings are not translated into concrete actions toward making positive change. In other words, it is not enough to understand the world, but it is also important to "do something about it."

Related to this broad critique is the question of student outputs that reflect experiential and challenge-driven learning. As we have also discussed in previous sections of this publication, it is critical to reconsider the traditional ways of assessing and evaluating learning. Already embedded in several methodologies for CIE, such as design thinking, is the making of prototypes, that is, early, rough versions of the final product or solutions envisaged to address the challenge given. In this section we position prototyping within a larger trend connected to a learning-by-doing or by making: the "maker movement."

According to The Maker Movement Manifesto,[64] *"making is fundamental to what it means to be human. We must make, create, and express ourselves to feel whole. There is something unique about making physical things...Making is closely connected to learning, particularly in creativity and innovation because the solution to a problem or the challenge is expected to take a material form. In addition, prototyping has also been closely connected to entrepreneurial learning, as it provides ways to test early ideas with potential customers and to better evaluate opportunities."[65]*

Making or prototyping has also been linked to the notion of "failing forward," or the idea that testing ideas and discovering their pitfalls early on is critical to the learning process and an important step toward their eventual success. Learning through making has been linked to students' potential as change makers and is perceived as an opportunity for learners to develop autonomy, collaboration and problem-solving abilities.[66] Relatedly, the maker movement has been praised for valuing "human passion, capability and the ability to make things happen and solve problems anywhere, anytime."[67] According to Blikstein,[68] digital fabrication and "making" in education are helping the "democratization of invention" by making accessible tasks and skills previously only in the hands of a few experts.

A study on engineering design projects at Stanford University and the Stockholm KTH Royal Institute of Technology has demonstrated that prototyping reinforces knowledge through social interaction. When different individuals join efforts to manifest their ideas in a physical form, they are also forced to share their thoughts in concrete ways and thus achieve a deeper connection to the knowledge accumulated through the literature or first-hand observations. In the authors' own words, prototypes "unlock cognitive association mechanisms related to visualization, prior experience, and interpersonal communication in ways that favour iterative learning between peers in the product development community."[69]

Although making and prototyping are well-established in fields such as engineering and design, it is only recently that these activities are being used in teaching and training CIE and are likely to become more relevant and important in the future as education is shifting toward more challenge-driven and immersive learning paradigms. Currently there are increasing numbers of makerspaces and fabrication labs on campuses and beyond, and there is a growing trend to transform library spaces into environments where students can be creative.[70]

One very successful example of makerspaces is Fab Labs. The idea of Fab Labs originated at MIT by Neil Gershenfeld, head of the Center for Bits and Atoms in his now famous course "How to make (almost) anything." The Center opened in 2001 and the course was designed to teach a small group of students how to use physical fabrication tools. When there was an overwhelming demand for the course, Gershenfeld began an outreach project supported by the National Science Foundation whereby he assembled a kit of equipment and materials worth about $70,000 and started with his colleagues the first fabrication lab or Fab Lab in the inner-city of Boston. The second FabLab was subsequently built in Ghana, and since then the model has spread all over the world.[71] According to the Fab Lab Network there are now around 2,000 Fab Labs in more than 149 countries "from community-based labs to advanced research centers [that] share the goal of democratizing access to the tools for technical invention."[72]

The Erasmus+ funded project "FabLabs: New Technologies in Adult Education"[73] has examined how fabrication spaces put forward a new model of learning that extends beyond the walls of traditional education institutions that at one time supported innovation and prototyping *and* built new environments for learning and building communities where people of all ages are able to be creative and build abilities based on their own interests. Explicit in the mission and philosophy of FabLabs is broadening access to previously unavailable or inaccessible tools and skills. As Diez (2012) has put it, FabLabs have become "platforms for citizen-based innovation" closely connected with the diverse but powerful Do-It-Yourself movement, "opening the same road maps in different spaces, garages or research centers."[74]

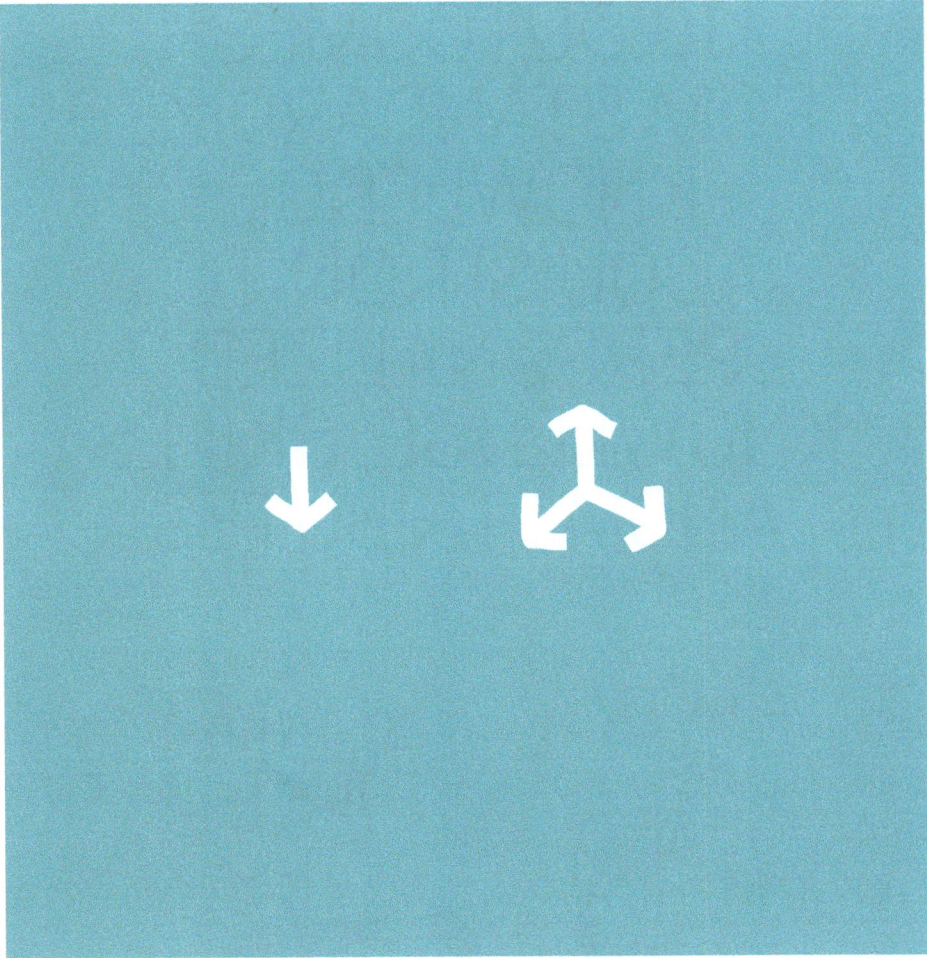

Overall, prototypes can function as guiding milestones, they show tangible progression or demonstrate specific features, and they enable systems integration, ensuring components and subsystems work together as planned.[75] The activities of building prototypes and communicating through prototypes are essential in ensuring effective learning experiences.

If a picture is worth a thousand words, a prototype is worth a thousand meetings. (IDEO.org)

10 OUTCOMES: FROM STANDARDIZED KNOWLEDGE ACQUISITION TO PERSONALIZED KNOWLEDGE, SKILLS AND ATTRIBUTES

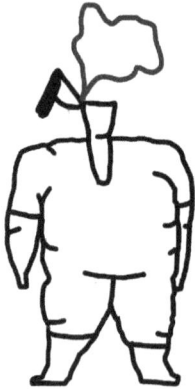

FROM
STANDARDIZED
KNOWLEDGE ACQUISITION...

TO
PERSONALIZED KNOWLEDGE,
SKILLS AND ATTRIBUTES

Learning outcomes are statements that describe the knowledge or skills that will be most valuable to the student now and in the future. In the past, we aimed to standardize knowledge acquisition, and all students were taught in similar ways. Now we need differentiated approaches to learning and to ensure learning outcomes that reflect personalized knowledge, skills, values, attitudes and meta-learning.

Trying to identify skills for the future of work, imagining jobs of the future and future work skills required for 2030 and beyond are the subject of many board discussions, conferences and policy reports. There is a clear need to assess which skills are required and how to train future students.[76] Several frameworks have been produced over the years detailing specific skills and competencies for the citizens of the future.[77] With a shift to lifelong learning, our definition of who the students are needs to be reconsidered: we are talking about learners of all ages through the entire duration of their lifetime (as captured in the shift on learners). Stephen Billett distinguished between lifelong learning and lifelong education[78] where learning is a personal process and education is an institutional act arising from and enacted by the social world. Lifelong learning should be built on the concept of an individual's vocations to guide the learning and development process.

In their report "Future Skills Framework 2030" the Foundation of Young Australians (FYA) highlighted that 70% of young people will need significant reskilling due to automation. FYA's CEO Jan Owen highlighted that:

> We must transform our approach to learning so that current and future workers have the skills employers need, and the cultural competencies required to thrive. This includes foundational skills, technical- or job-specific skills, career management capabilities and enterprise skills – often called 'soft' or '21st century' skills.

The World Economic Forum Report on the future of work indicates "By one popular estimate, 65% of children entering primary school today will ultimately end up working in completely new job types that don't yet exist."

Therefore, the ability to anticipate and prepare for future skill requirements, job content and the aggregate effect on employment is increasingly critical for businesses, governments and individuals to fully seize the opportunities presented by these trends – and to mitigate undesirable outcomes[79] (WEF, 2016). This involves:

> supporting reskilling and upskilling in better ways... I think this is all just an outcome of the shifting of the workplace and shifting of expectations within work. (Dan Sleeman, Head of Product and Education, RMIT Activator, Australia)

Our research shows that institutions across many levels globally recognize the need to focus on the future skills, sometimes referred to as competency-based learning and 21st-century skills, and start to incorporate these shifts into their programs.

First, we see a shift from developing job-ready skills to skills that will help with any future upskilling. As one of the Minerva students points out,

> we need to give people the skills to upskill, rather than just giving them new knowledge, because by the time we give them the new knowledge and build all of those courses, we've already moved on to like three iterations of new technological advances.

There is also an increasing recognition for anticipatory and future-oriented skills, future literacy

> we generate the risk-takers of the future who push the boundaries a little bit further. (Clare Stead, CEO Oliiki, UK)

The goal is not to ensure that expert-based knowledge is memorized but to enforce the capability of an individual to be a self-directed learner.

Second, as highlighted in several chapters, there is an increasing emphasis on learning by doing. Few jobs will remain static and with the pace of technological change, it will be necessary to constantly learn to be successful in the work environment, to change roles, to create a business. To support the development of skills and thrive in complex and ambiguous work environments, learning by doing or experiential learning helps students to explore, experiment and reflect upon concepts and "ways of being" in unstructured settings.[80] This requires the development of capabilities and the facilitation of creative thinking in collaboration. Authors demonstrate that learning placements in entrepreneurial environments can play an important role in contextualizing and driving learning processes. As a facilitator in the New Zealand Future Work collective, Susan Basterfield pointed out that

> every meeting, you can practice everything, you can practice your listening skills, you can practice your critical thinking skills, you can practice your facilitation skills, you can practice what it's like to reserve judgment by asking questions, instead of jumping to solutions, right?

In particular, alongside technological and social change, universities need to nurture start-ups and entrepreneurial mindsets and should develop an active entrepreneurial ecosystem to help students develop their knowledge of current and future technologies, skill sets and work industry trends.[81]

Third, many institutions try to position themselves as addressing grand global challenges or SDGs (see chapter Subject Matter for more details). This has led some institutions to focus on developing skills needed to address global challenges: skills for the future that will empower students to develop their entrepreneurial skills and innovate solutions to environmental and social challenges.

These shifts emphasize the importance of system thinkers, moving from a specialist to generalist curriculum:

> *These need to be very well-educated people who have systems thinking capabilities, and who have depth in many things. They're not over specialized but they are also not generalists. They are people who can connect the dots and are systems thinkers - we need more people who think in systems and not in silos. I think what we saw in the last 20 years is a trend to over specialization to some extent.* (Susann Roth, ADB, Philippines)

There is still a lot of debate on what skills need to be embedded on future driven curricula. While our research acknowledges the importance of soft and hard skills, we somehow see the need to go beyond them:

> *One of the things that are often not mandated in the core curriculum is this something beyond the skills, which is personality, dispositions, habits of mind, value systems, ethics, and morality.* (Raya Bidshahri, Founder & CEO, School of Humanity, UAE)

With the shift to soft skills and beyond, we think that technical, digital and data literacy skills remain important:

> *I would say we really need to make sure people have technical foundations because I can see this now in this whole COVID discussion, how much wrong information and wrong interpretation of evidence and so on is going around. So I do believe we need to have very strong foundations and techniques, the technical foundations for how things work.*

Overall, to account for learning outcomes that prepare students for the future, there is:
- the need to support the development of skills (soft, hard and beyond) as a lifelong learning journey
- the need to finally acknowledge the soft skills in the job descriptions
- the need to focus on designing holistic learning experiences by fusing these skills: digital, systems thinking and problem solving
- the need to redesign curricula to incorporate future shifts/demands

Overall, learning outcomes need to reflect economic, social and environmental challenges and help learners develop deep competencies and cultivate habits that will continue to be valuable long after graduation.

> *To develop a complete mind: study the science of art; study the art of science. Learn how to see. Realize that everything connects to everything else.* (Leonardo da Vinci)

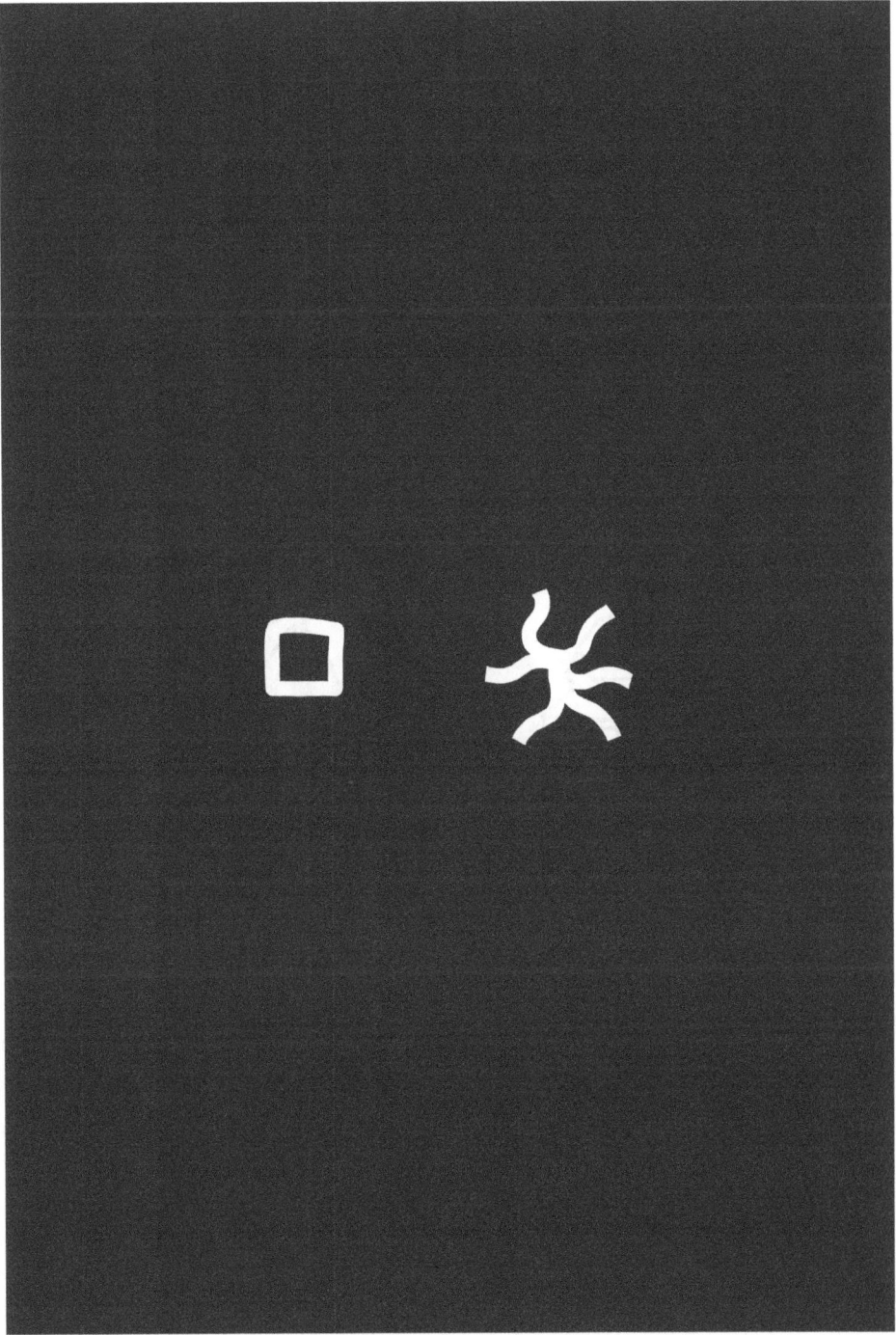

11 IMPACT: FROM INSTITUTIONAL TO SOCIETAL

FROM
INSTITUTIONAL...

TO
TO SOCIETAL

Creating relevance for the academic world and reaching into the world are the most common purposes of impact practices in HEIs. Collaboration between universities and industry is one approach to close this gap and to improve innovation by facilitating the flow of knowledge and experience across the sectors. The aim is to enhance knowledge exchange between academic and industry domains.

In the past, it seemed natural to follow a threefold approach where research, teaching and practice are understood to be independent dimensions of knowledge acquisition. As a result, innovation theory and innovation in practice differ substantially. In research, this gap is called the "relevance gap." Some even go as far as to suggest that "most of what management researchers do utterly fails to resonate with management practice."[82] What practitioners want are roadmaps for how to do things and insights into how to implement best practices. They want simple ideas, and simple "lessons learned." Traditionally, universities teach theoretical models, academics publish research on what practitioners should do, not on how they can do so.

Focus on research impact is increasingly recognized as a professional development need within academia.[83] There is a proliferation of initiatives which aim to build researchers' capabilities to attain the impact from their research and teaching. For example, multiple universities develop research impact case studies to showcase the work that researchers are doing. These research impact case studies offer researcher and practitioner stories, reflections, and tips on (sometimes failed) efforts to generate research impact,[84] including challenges in working with stakeholders.[85]

The impact of learning is as important as the research impact for HEIs. The impact of learning helps teachers and institutions to better understand their impact on student learning. Exploring relationships between education, teaching and student achievement is a complex task that should include the complexity of teaching, the number of different approaches to teacher education, the challenges associated with measuring teacher knowledge and teacher effectiveness, and the multiple mediators that operate in the study of teaching and learning.[86]

In practice, there is a shift toward more vocational and practice-based learning. This has resulted in new offerings by HEIs including nano- and micro-degrees, competency-based programs and expanded online options.

Existing forms of university-industry collaboration such as joint ventures, networks, knowledge alliances, co-creation labs, open innovation labs, accelerators, joint workshops and projects are typically used to seek practical relevance in teaching and research. Makerspaces and on-campus accelerators bring students together from different disciplines and link them to industry through co-design and learning-by-doing practices.

To embed more impactful education, we need to train students on the importance of translation between scientists and practitioners as well as the techniques to do so to close the gap between both worlds. This can be achieved by bringing more practitioners to the university (lecturing practitioner) and/or more academics into practice (e.g., academic trainers and part-time researchers). Intensifying ethnographic research methods, for example, in-depth case studies, action research, participatory research and engaged scholarship could also extend a continuous exchange between industry and academia. Researchers should transfer their research results into praxis and publish more scientific studies working on relevant challenges from and for industry. This is already the case in certain executive MBA programs where students pay per semester and decide on the length of their studies.

But do the existing initiatives really meet the rising need for education to solve society-relevant problems? Is the traditional semester-based structure sufficient to cater to collaboration needs from industry and society at large? Adapting the fixed university curriculum of two semesters into a more flexible collaboration-emphasizing structure might also help to adapt to industry needs.

Seeking practical relevance and reaching into the real world to ensure social legitimacy needs to be combined with developing new research and learning cultures that embed futures literacy. Futures literacy capability is crucial for teachers and researchers to envision their profession and their role in society. To develop a futures literacy capability, it is important to emphasize the collective imaginary around the futures of impact, fostering critical reflexivity and experimentation, and ensuring responsible, ethical research impact.[87]

> Learning of the highest value extends well beyond measurable dimensions. It can't be fitted into any curriculum or evaluated by any test. It is activated by experiences which develop our humanity. It teaches us to be our best selves. (Laura Grace Weldon)

12 EVALUATION: FROM ONE-DIMENSIONAL TO MULTIDIMENSIONAL

FROM
ONE-DIMENSIONAL...

TO
TO MULTIDIMENSIONAL

Demonstrating that the desired outputs, outcomes and impact were successfully achieved is a critical yet difficult task. The shifts in the learning landscape reported in this publication fundamentally challenge the traditional ways of evaluation and assessment. When education is driven by the acquisition of information on a specific subject contained in textbooks, then assessments can be easily standardized and scaled in the form of exams. However, as in the case of CIE, when outputs include physical artifacts, outcomes are competence-focused and the impact is presumed to reach society-at-large, and so evaluation becomes extremely complicated. Furthermore, evaluation needs to carefully consider the collaborative and self-determined nature of learning, as well as the learning journey itself.

According to Mulgan and colleagues, any assessment of learning outcomes must begin with the setting of two critical parameters: (1) the scope of learning, that is, *what* is it that a student of a particular subject/domain should learn? (2) the mode of assessment, that is, *how* can we ascertain the extent to which the student has actually acquired the requisite knowledge of the subject/domain?[88] Importantly, assessments should have a clear value to the learners, and these values should be clearly communicated to them. As another report aptly puts it, assessments should be "educational experiences themselves, ... composed of 'worthy' authentic learning tasks" and should be accompanied by "supportive and actionable feedback based on the results."[89]

Some universities have already been experimenting with assessments.[90] For example, Stanford University introduced a "PBL model" that denotes Problem, Project, Product, Process and People-Based Learning.[91] This model uses a cross-disciplinary knowledge framework to grade engineering students partially on the basis of their understanding of other related fields as well as on other soft factors such as teamwork, presentation of the product and process and system integration thinking.

Similarly, McMaster Medical School actively discourages "learning for the test" and instead encourages a collaborative learning environment. It has developed an approach defined as "GRADE" (Grading of Recommendations, Assessment, Development and Evaluation) that is based on grading of the quality of evidence and was developed in a collaborative effort by "methodologists, guideline developers, clinicians and other interested members with the aim of developing and implementing a common, transparent and sensible approach to grading the quality of evidence and strength of recommendations in health care."[92] Such approaches, however, are not yet widespread.

To maintain quality control in fields with such highly context-specific knowledge, skills and competencies, the job market is likely to see a shift away from traditional examinations toward what can be called evidence-based learning. Technological advancements make it increasingly possible "to evaluate how people think and not just what they know." For this purpose, tests can be "designed to measure such things as whether applicants can work in teams, communicate and make good decisions."[93]

In our research we identified one framework that is particularly helpful in capturing the multidimensional aspects of learning involved in evaluating creativity, innovation, entrepreneurship programs. Developed by Charles Fadel and colleagues[94] this framework considers the following four dimensions: (1) knowledge: "what we know and understand" (Interdisciplinarity, Traditional, Modern, Themes); (2) skills: "how we use what we know" (Creativity, Critical Thinking, Communication and Collaboration); (3) character: "how we behave and engage in the world (Mindfulness, Curiosity, Courage, Resilience, Ethics and Leadership) and (4) meta-learning: "how we reflect and adapt" (Metacognition, Growth Mindset).

Building on this report and drawing on our empirical material and additional literature, we present in Table 3 some aspects that we believe could be used in the evaluation of CIE learning programs. We find the OECD's conceptual framework on attitudes and values, in which these are defined as "principles and beliefs that influence one's choices, judgements, behaviors and actions on the path toward individual, societal and environmental well-being"[95] particularly useful to consider in the design, delivery and evaluation of CIE programs. Needless to say, these aspects have to be carefully woven into the learning journey and be evident in the delivery and outputs expected. Although evaluation is presented as the final element in our learning landscape, it is absolutely critical and there is much need for further research on this topic.

> *Tell me and I forget. Teach me and I remember. Involve me and I learn.* (Benjamin Franklin)

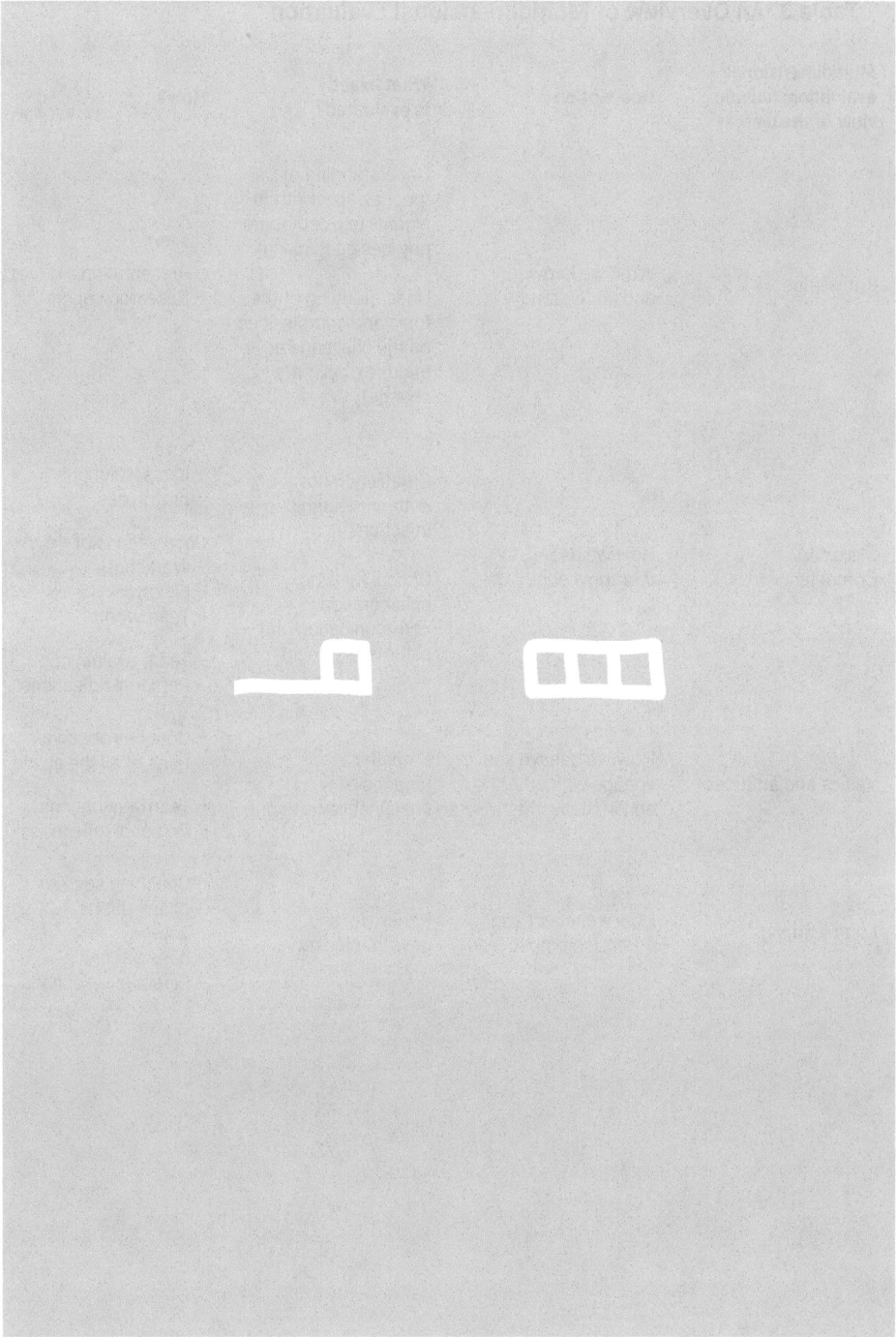

Table 3. An Overview of Multidimensional Evaluation

Multidimensional evaluation; holistic view of the learner	Description	What exactly is evaluated?	How?
Knowledge	What we know and understand	Understanding of CIE theories and methodologies (e.g., ethnography, design thinking) Understanding of the topic and complexities on the challenge at hand (e.g., climate change)	– Presentations – Research papers
Skills and Competencies	How we use this knowledge	Creativity, innovation, entrepreneurship in action Critical thinking, collaboration, communication and self-management	Above + – Ideas/solutions prototypes *Observations* of: – Workshops – Fieldwork – Teamwork – Team evaluations – Personal reflections
Values and attitudes	How we behave and engage with others and in the world	Empathy, responsibility, sustainability and grit	– Coaches observations of all the above – Team evaluations – Personal reflections
Meta-learning	How we reflect and adapt; learning to learn	Reflexivity and growth mindset	– Coaching session observations – Journey observations – Personal reflections

PART II

SNAPSHOTS INTO THE FUTURE

As part of the Vision project, we had the privilege to interview 136 people involved in initiatives that are transforming their learning landscapes and showcasing the shifts described above. Many of our interviewees gave examples of other amazing programs and projects. In this section we capture some of these from across the globe to illustrate how changes are currently happening within the traditional higher education sector, as well as corporate, lifelong learning and EdTech spaces.

We succinctly present these initiatives and position them across the 12 critical elements we presented in Part I, as illustrated in the "spider web" below. Some of the snapshots exemplify a shift of one specific element, while others tackle many at once. The examples are chosen and presented by different members of the Vision consortium.

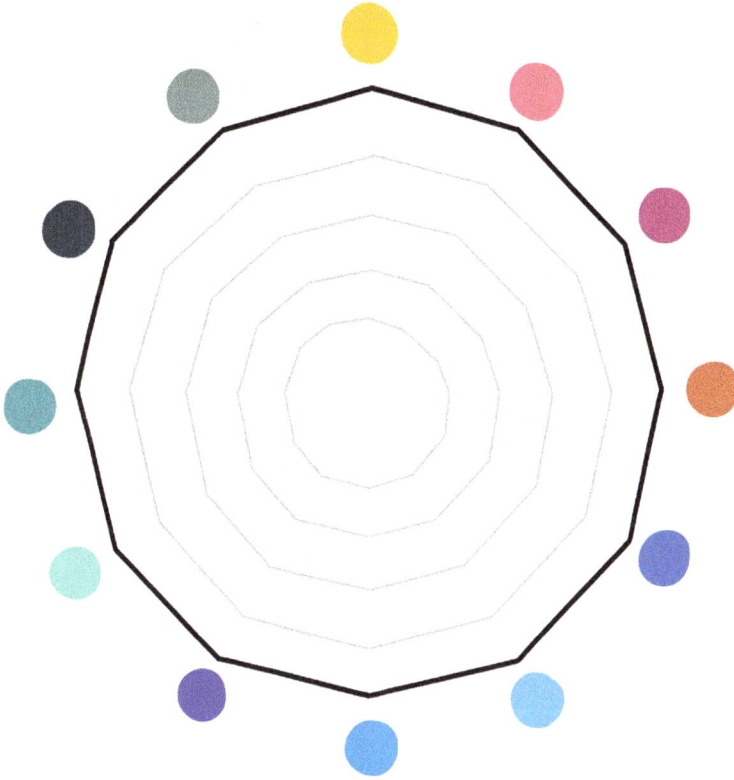

PILARS OF LEARNING

- 🟡 TEACHER
- 🔴 STUDENT
- 🟣 SUBJECT MATTER
- 🟠 SPACE

LEARNING JOURNEY

- 🔵 STYLE
- 🔵 PROCESS
- 🔵 PHYSICAL MATERIAL ARTIFACTS
- 🟣 DIGITAL TECHNOLOGY

LEARNING RESULTS

- 🟢 EVALUATION
- 🟢 OUTPUTS
- ⚫ OUTCOMES
- 🟢 IMPACT

Some of the organizations presented collaborate with each other and we believe that insights can be generated across these institutions. We hope that some of these snapshots can be a source of inspiration on how you can grapple with the shifting learning landscape today, and introduce new activities and actions that can enhance learning for CIE. This will make your initiatives future-ready now.

Higher Education Institutions:
- Minerva, US
- Fusion Point, Spain
- Worms University of Applied Science, Germany
- Fresenius University of Applied Sciences, OnlinePlus, Germany
- Minneapolis College of Art and Design, US

Corporate Education and Lifelong Learning:
- Future of Work Collective, New Zealand
- SEB Growth Program, Latvia
- Vodafone Foundation, Germany
- TÜV NORD GROUP, Digital Academy, Germany
- The College of Extraordinary Experiences, Poland

EdTech:
- Tech Futures Lab, New Zealand
- The School of Humanity, UAE
- Bangalore, India
- Bakpax, US
- Classe Investigation, France

HIGHER EDUCATION INSTITUTIONS

Minerva School
Presented by Olga Kokshagina

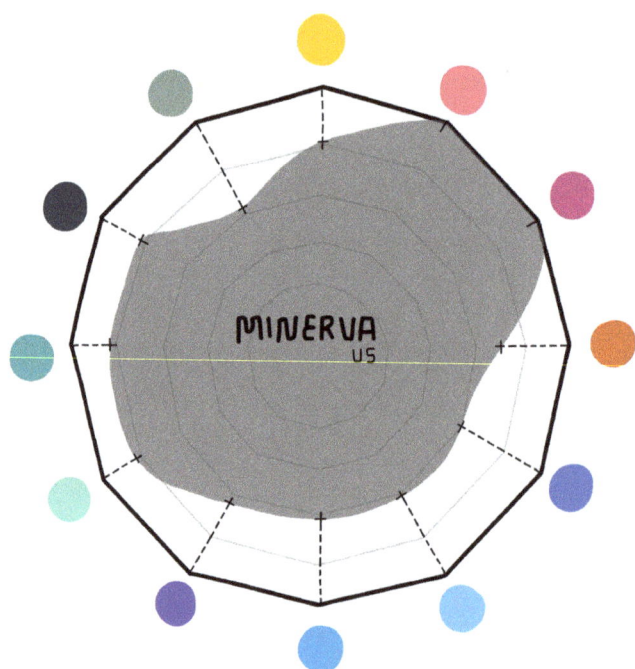

Minerva is a venture-backed Silicon Valley initiative which was founded in 2012 by Ben Nelson. Based on the science of learning in a wide range of areas, including the study of memory, perception, comprehension, learning and reasoning, Minerva has partnered with the Keck Graduate Institute to create a comprehensive approach to developing durable, broadly applicable skills to help people succeed in school, the workforce and society at large. Different learning principles are embedded and classified as *Think it Through*: the more you think something through, paying attention to what you are doing, the more likely you are later to remember it and *Make and Use Associations*: associations not only help us organize material so that it is easy to store in memory but also give us the hooks that will allow us later to recall it.

Counted among its innovative aspects are no lectures, faculty buildings or exams. All teaching is done through online video classes and teachers never present for more than a few minutes to ensure dialogue among students and act as facilitators and coaches. Less than a decade after its creation, Minerva serves as a model for other institutions.

All students at Minerva work around the so-called first Habits of Mind and Foundational Concepts (HCs) that underpin curriculum, course and lesson design, as well as the ongoing evaluation of learner performance. These foundational concepts are thinking critically, thinking creatively, communicating effectively and interacting effectively. These HCs are further divided into concepts. For example, "interacting effectively" involves resolving critical problems, interacting with complex systems, negotiating and persuading, and working with others. Furthermore, each concept is associated with a set of hashtags (i.e., #multipleagents; #levelsofanalysis; #emergentpoperties; #multiplecauses, #networks for interacting with complex systems).

As one of the students interviewed indicated, for #multiplecauses you would consider "how in a business context, how every single customer is unique, you know how they might have different expectations based on their backgrounds, obviously, different expectations of price, different expectations of, you know, delivery speeds, things like that different communication styles." The curriculum is built around the quantification of soft or enterprise skills, as well as hard skills and competencies. For every project students are engaged in, they reflect on the skills that they apply and keep track of the hashtags applied in each activity. The goal is to build *transversal skills*.

Tests and exams where students are evaluated continuously are considered obsolete. Instead, students reflect on how they apply different HCs. Those are collected over four years and grades are finalized only at the end of the final year. The reason for the grades being finalized only during the fourth year relates to the so-called transfers. Transfers occur when students use the hashtags from other disciplines. For example, when a student studies arts and humanities and uses data analysis techniques, she must include a hashtag on #correlation or #data-visualization to reflect on the origins of different methods and techniques used (*Think it Through* principles).

The framework allows students to reflect on skills applied in each context and promotes interdisciplinarity and discipline-free learning that prepares students to navigate future shifts. In terms of learning styles, the school promotes active learning where a video platform enables teachers to monitor how learners contribute to class discussions and group work. Everything that students do is actively monitored. This might raise privacy issues.

SKILLS
ACTIVELY MONITORED
NO FACULTY BUILDING BUT ON LINE
INTERDISCIPLINARY
TEACHER AS COACHER
#MULTIPLEAGENTS
#LEVELSOFANALYSIS
#EMERGENTPOPERTIES
#MULTIPLECAUSES
TRANSVERSAL SKILLS
HABITS OF MIND AND FOUNDATIONAL CONCEPTS – HCs
CURRICULUM
COURSE
LESSON DESIGN
ONGOING EVALUATION
1° > > 2° > > 3° > > 4°
YEAR
NO EXAMS BUT HOW TO APPLY DIFFERENT HCs

Fusion Point
Presented by Kyriaki Papageorgiou

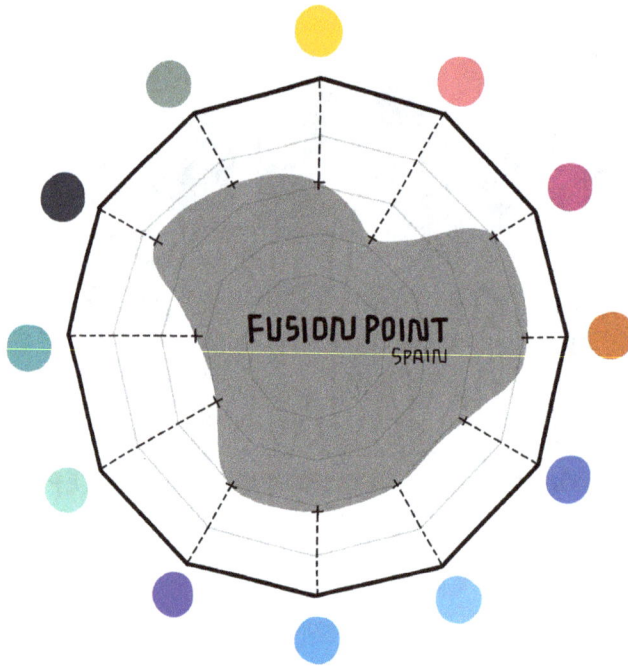

Fusion Point is an initiative that aims to find innovative solutions to real-life challenges through interdisciplinary work in education and research. It brings together students from business and law from ESADE, engineering and technology from the Polytechnic University of Catalonia (UPC) and design from IED Barcelona Design University. The three schools first came together in 2014 within the context of a course that originated in CERN and formalized their collaboration in 2018 under the name Fusion Point. This is an homage, in a way, to the physics experiment that first brought them together.

Fusion Point is part of the Design Factory Global Network (DFGN) and its design and creation was directly linked with Aalto University in Finland, which has become a reference point of positive reform for multidisciplinary research and education. More concretely, Aalto University has spearheaded a model for innovation and learning through its Design Factory that features a physical space with flexible teaching spaces, prototyping facilities and co-working spaces where multidisciplinary teams can convene for project-based courses that tackle challenges provided by external sponsors.[96]

Fusion Point shares the core mission of DFGN "to build a new kind of passion-based learning culture" and support collaboration and co-creation across disciplines between students, researchers and practitioners. Similar to other design factories, Fusion Point is also a co-creation platform "promoting a culture of experimentation and collaboration with diverse stakeholders."[97] In addition, Fusion Point has a dedicated space for work at the Esade Sant Cugat campus that is inspired by the Aalto design factory, with its flexible spaces.

One of the signature courses of Fusion Point is Challenged-Based Innovation (CBI), a course that originated and is grounded at CERN with the explicit goal to link CERN science and expertise to address societal challenges. Fusion Point has developed its own unique version of the CBI course that formulates the challenges given to the students around the UN Sustainable Development Goals (SDGs). By the end of the course, the students will have developed a functional prototype. The course normally runs from September to mid-December and students work in small multidisciplinary teams (5–6 people). Over a period of 15 weeks, there are weekly meetings with workshops, seminars and coaching sessions. Each team is assigned to three coaches, one from each school. The students travel together to CERN three times during the course for a total of 15 days, where they present their final prototypes during the final trip.

In addition to CBI, Fusion Point has developed different kinds of courses that share the same five core elements: they are: challenge driven, multidisciplinary, experiential, experimental and aim to be socially relevant and impactful beyond academia. Each program initiated by Fusion Point is an experiment itself, used to implement and test novel tools and approaches to generate creative ideas and practical innovative solutions.

Worms University of Applied Sciences

Presented by Carina Leue-Bensch

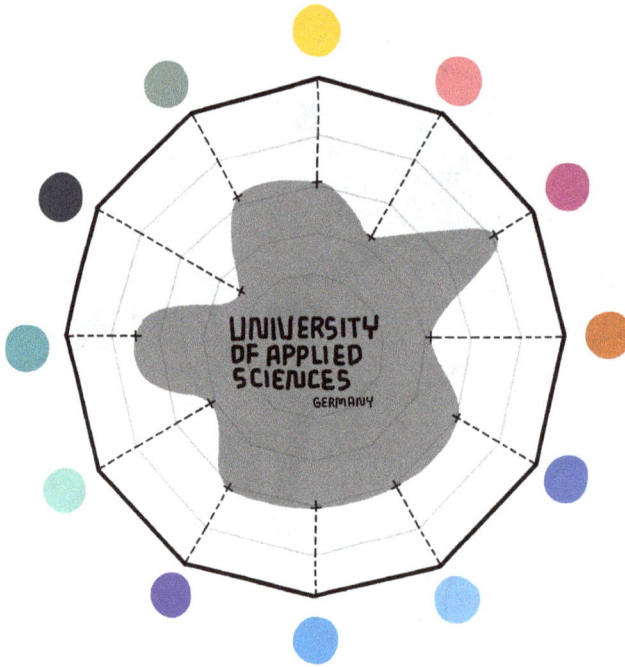

Worms University of Applied Sciences has three faculties: Informatics, Tourism and Travel Management, and Business Administration. It has approximately 3,700 students. In order to adapt to the needs of industry partners and to give students more practical experience, the Worms University of Applied Sciences reduced, student presence time from 15 to 12 weeks per semester for all "traditional" courses, such as Global Trade Management, Digital Business Management or Entrepreneurship, in their International Business Administration program (IBA). IBA learners can either apply as dual students with a direct link to industry partners, combining theoretical knowledge with practical experience in their partner company, or learners could join the traditional stream without an industry partnership.

In practical terms, after a concentrated 12-week lecture period, dual students normally start their applied work mission in their companies. Students of the traditional stream, however, will spend three more weeks at the university working in industry-related interdisciplinary block modules. These block seminars enable new forms of learning and teaching in which students can focus on a topic area and work continuously in teams to achieve their goals. Within the block modules, Boot Camp-Like and Summer School formats can be realized in a more application-oriented way. This way the university reinforces university-industry collaboration and enables students to relate and focus their theoretical knowledge to practical experiences and skills. In order to ensure a strong link to industry and relate their courses to the most recent industry challenges, the university is also intensifying the employment of "lecturing practitioners," or "practicing lecturers" in a way that their lecturers and professors are incentivized to stay engaged in an industry position next to their teaching.

Furthermore, the university's new master program "Entrepreneurship" brings together students with diverse backgrounds and cultures to collaborate in various projects. Bringing local industry contacts and their recent problems, the students develop solutions collaboratively. During the course projects, there is an ongoing collaboration with the companies to ensure user-centered learning experience and to explore and validate different directions. The final outcome of the projects is prototypes, which are pitched to the partner companies. This way the students not only learn about the theoretical concepts of an innovation process, but also apply it in practice.

In addition to working on industry driven challenges, the students are also encouraged to think about building their own businesses. As part of a specific Innovation Management course as well as the university's own "Gründerwerkstatt," teachers act as coaches and mentors to discuss and shape the students' business ideas. Students can also work on their prototypes using the makerspace facilities on campus and build their own business plans.

Some ideas bring the opportunity to include a company from the very beginning. These ideas could grow, that is, out of the interdisciplinary study format "team-oriented project" where students develop an actionable concept and prototype in eight weeks. Under time pressure and in a competitive manner, students must build a team, get in professional contact with possible customers and finally present their concepts in a convincing way to a large audience. In fact, several concept ideas have successfully emerged as new startups from this study format accompanied by the start-up office and professors acting as mentors and sparring partners.

Fresenius University of Applied Sciences, OnlinePlus

Presented by Rajnish Tiwari

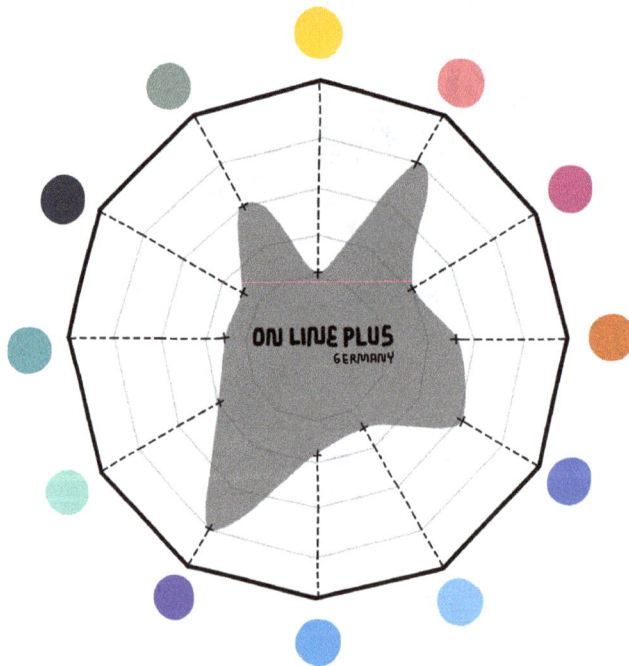

Hochschule Fresenius ("Fresenius University of Applied Sciences," HSF) is a private German university founded in 1848. In 2016, HSF set up a new faculty named OnlinePlus (OLP) which offers courses in business administration, engineering, psychology, healthcare, and media & communication management. Some of the core objectives of OLP are inclusive access to education and offerings of multidisciplinary courses under one roof. It has introduced an innovative "Mixed Mode" format that has been formally recognized by the Ministry of Higher Education, Research, Science and the Arts of the Federal State of Hessen.

More specifically, the "Mixed Mode" format focuses on the learner by allowing students to engage in individual, flexible and permeable lifelong learning. As a university press release puts itL, it is "a unique study model in which students can individually combine their studies from online and classroom courses – depending on their learning preferences, time commitments or life situation. The study programme thus adapts to the student's life and not vice versa."[98]

Students can study bachelor, master, certificate or micro-degree courses in full-time or part-time formats. The mode of learning for any given course module is variable, and it can be face-to-face, eLearning or blended/hybrid formats. The Mixed Mode courses are offered monthly and are not dependent on a fixed semester cycle. Online course material is supplemented with online seminars that can be attended voluntarily by students. Students are also largely free to choose between online 24x7 examinations and in-class examinations at any of the six study centers in Berlin, Cologne, Dusseldorf, Hamburg, Munich and Wiesbaden. The idea is to enable "anytime, anywhere" education.

The Mixed Mode also significantly alters the role of the teacher in the concerned courses. While knowledge relevant for the course curriculum can be directly acquired by the student by going through the lecture material and other content specifically developed for the course and made available online, classes in physical formats focus on the creation and transmission of tacit knowledge and soft skills. Classes take place in the form of seminars that make use of problem-based learning, where the teacher takes the role of a facilitator. The eLearning platform of OLP allows interactive learning and connects with fellow students and faculty members spread across the world, thus also allowing global access and collaboration. A core objective followed by OLP is societal inclusion that is targeted through affordable access to lifelong learning. Many of the students of OLP are part-time students that work full-time and in many cases are spread globally. It is not unusual to have young German-speaking students located in the United States, Greece and Spain all joining an online seminar.

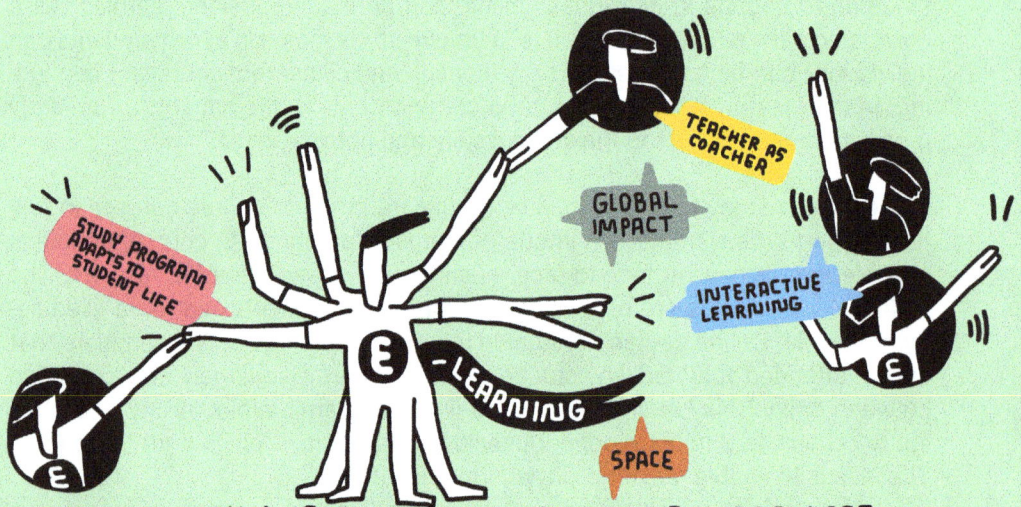

Minneapolis College of Art and Design

Presented by Olga Kokshagina

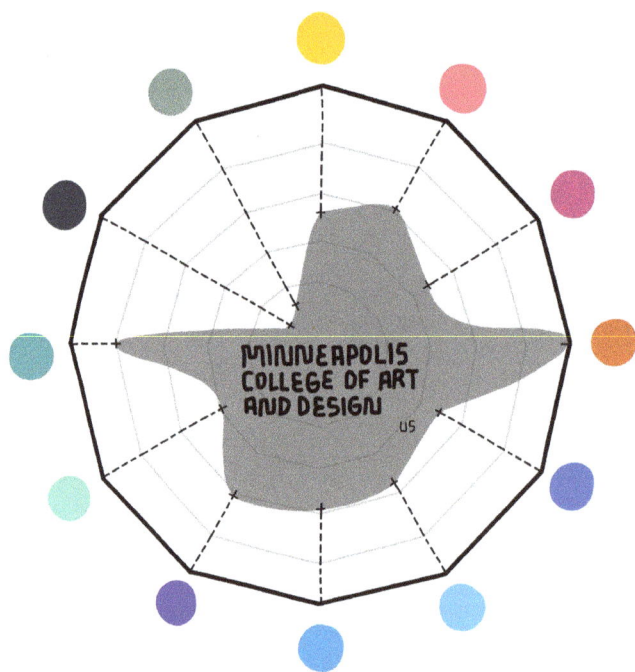

Established in 1886, Minneapolis College of Art and Design (MCAD) is a private college specializing in the visual arts and located in Minneapolis, Minnesota. MCAD currently enrolls approximately 800 students. The college is involved in all levels of education: undergraduate, graduate, certificates in biomimicry, design foundations, teaching art and design online; continuing education for pre-college, adults and teachers. Its vision: "MCAD emboldens creative leaders to collaboratively transform society through equity, empathy, and imagination."

When it comes to using technologies to design better education experiences, MCAD was the first art and design school to offer an online MFA (Master in Fine Arts), which embraces accessibility and allows people to be an integrated part of the college community without needing to be on campus. During the COVID-19 pandemic, MCAD decided to transition to 100% online delivery. The faculty was able to do small group demonstrations and small group conversations in class and was able to include students who couldn't be present to benefit from it. The online environment also brought challenges in teaching creative professionals where physical tools like 3D printers and CNC machines could not be used in fully online environments making prototyping physical objects harder. Nevertheless, going forward, these constraints can potentially lead to new ways of designing and collaborating online when one cannot rely on traditional tools. This leads to important shifts in the role of physical materials, artifacts and other equipment as well as styles and processes of learning.

Subject matter and formats are changing as well, introducing more and more interdisciplinary programs. For example, MCAD is the only college in the USA that has an undergraduate major in arts entrepreneurship. They are experimenting with types of degrees as well, providing opportunities for learning beyond the established four-year programs, acknowledging the problems of accreditation that accompany non-traditional degrees.

Finally, MCAD has an explicit focus on soft skills, embedding principles of experiential learning. For example, the Design Department at MCAD "provides a rigorous learning experience that challenges, inspires, and educates students majoring in comic art, graphic design, and illustration. Innovative creative thinking and form-making are equally nurtured within all programs through a robust studio practice, cross-disciplinary curricula, and a productive engagement with both traditional and emerging technologies."[99]

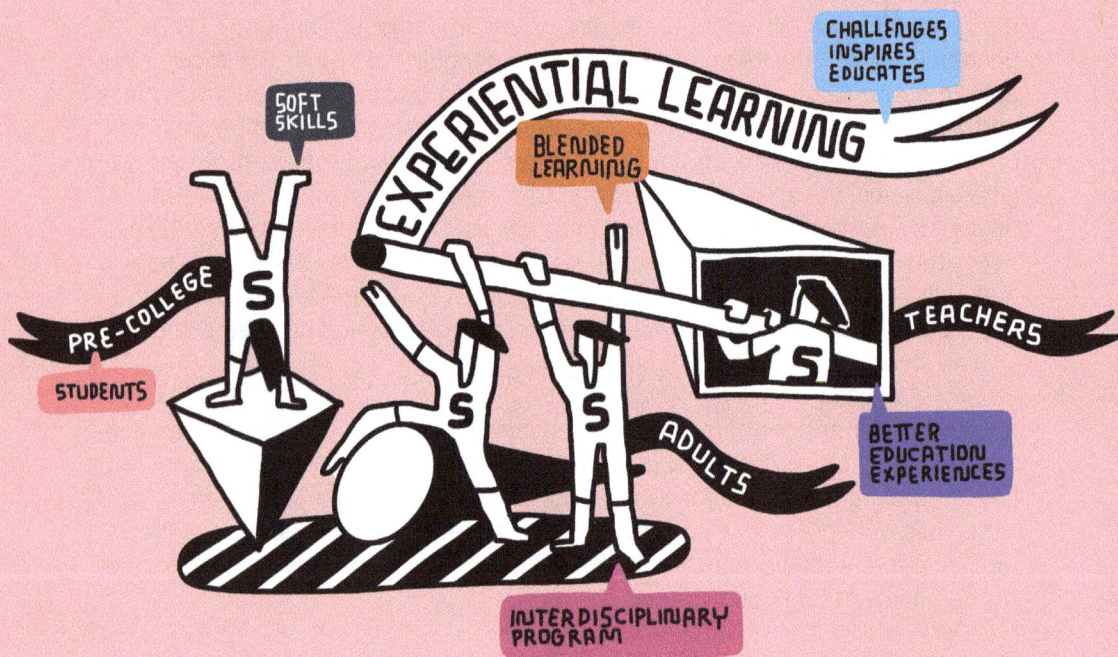

CORPORATE EDUCATION

Future of Work Collective
Presented by Olga Kokshagina

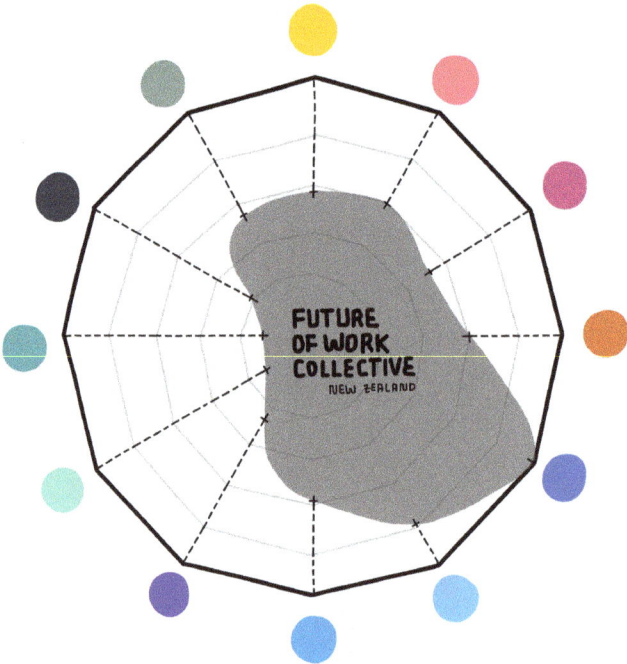

PART II

The Future of Work Collective is an innovative self-managed boutique consultancy of senior corporate professionals who radically reinvented their own ways of working. As stated on the website: "Our purpose is to reinvent corporate culture and leadership to innovate brighter futures." This organization constantly experiments with new styles and processes of lifelong learning in the corporate space. For example, they have an online leadership development program that uses new ways of connecting, ideating, sharing and working together. The impact of this project is "digital uplift and appreciation of leaders, cross-national-network connection, collective intelligence augmentation." The Future of work Collective proposes lifelong learning labs that aim to grow capability and engagement through immersive experiences. In these experiences, the goal is "to cultivate micro-practices and principles that engage the whole self, build connection and harness the differences that make us all unique. Everything is built on trust, voluntary participation and collective intelligence."[100]

Creativity is one of the core guiding principles of this collective, alongside empathy, integrity, and systems thinking. In addition, special attention is given to creating ground for collaboration and learning by doing. In the words of Sandra Otto, one of its co-founders, *"Key to this experiential learning is psychological safety. And we call that trust. And the key tool that we use is what we call the authentic check-in."* The latter means starting meetings with check-ins where each participant gets a turn to briefly share what is happening in "their world"– what they are thinking, feeling, and wanting at that moment. This helps to create a safe space where everyone can share their authentic feelings and thoughts. Even the space for learning is organized in a specific way to organize for collaboration, whereby instead of sitting in desks, like in a traditional workplace or university classroom, people sit in circles, resembling more "a kindergarten or indigenous environment of circles and talking sticks."[101]

For the Future Work Collective, learning is a journey, and the goal is to provide people with tools and resources so that students can "bring their learning home" or "making it home in yourself" (an inspirational framing of the word "homework"). But the emphasis on the self and personalized learning does not necessarily mean egocentrism. As the name itself implies, this initiative adopts an approach that emphasizes collectivism, recognizing that for a self-directed lifelong journey one needs both personal drive and support from peers.

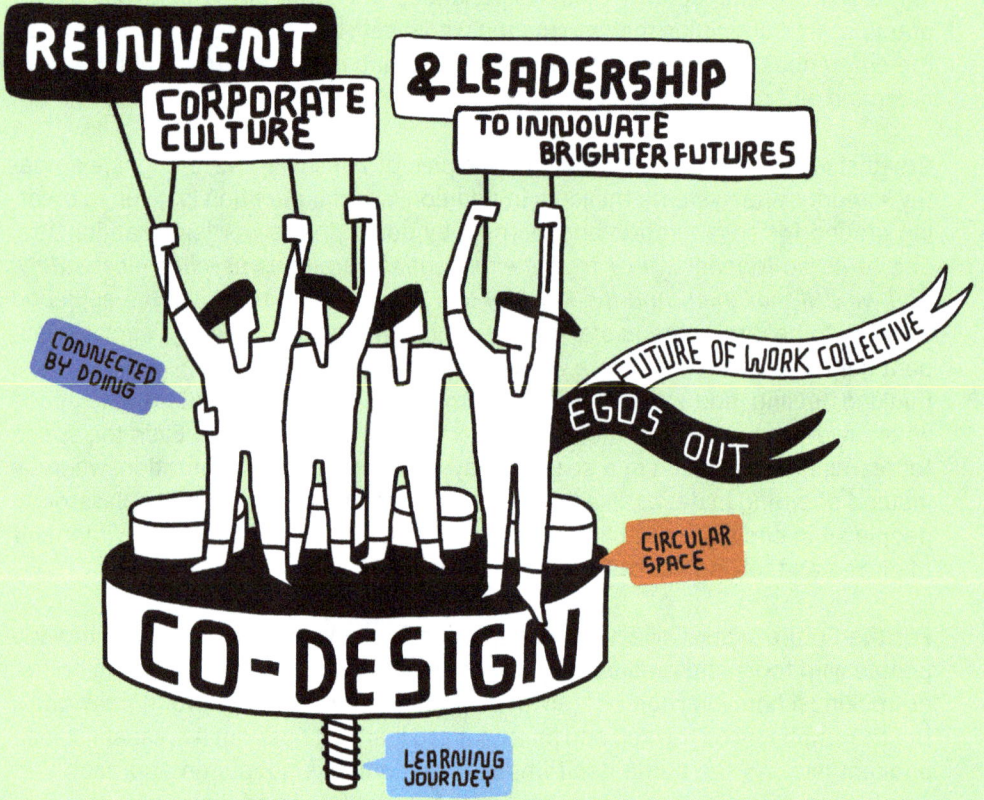

Growth Program, SEB Bank

Presented by Beata Lavrinoviča[102]

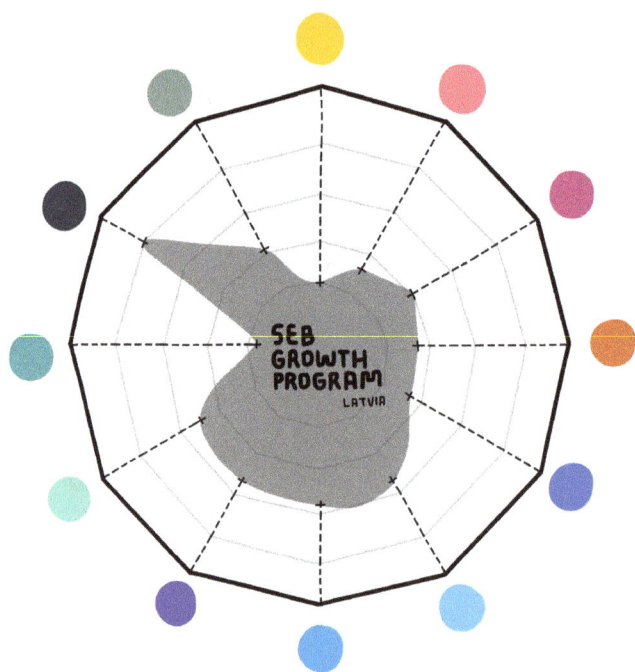

The SEB Growth Program is a bank-lead business accelerator for ambitious small-to medium-sized enterprises (SMEs) to grow their business 10-fold, not 10%. SEB is one of the largest banks in the Baltics which attracts both local and international business experts, involves companies in the implementation of practical tasks and provides individual support. First launched in 2017, the focus of the program is on the development of business knowledge and skills, with an emphasis on innovation, as well as other important 21st-century attitudes and values, such as sustainability and growth thinking. The goal of this program is to help entrepreneurs better understand and apply lean start-up, human-centered approaches and rapid experimentation approaches in their business processes, as well as improve their communication and management skills.

The program is divided into three phases. First is the selection phase when SMEs with innovative development ideas and growth potential are invited to an intense one-day bootcamp, at the end of which 15 participant teams are selected to take part in the program. The intensive phase follows with a four-month long period of bi-weekly public lectures, ideation sessions to align teams' plans and set the focus for the program, closed workshops and individual mentoring sessions with the experts to clarify uncertainties and focus on the specific needs of each company. The third phase is the 100-day project implementation, which starts with the focus on teams' individual work and regular progress reviews. The program concludes with a demo day when all participants pitch their progress.

The SEB Growth Program allows participants to step out of their daily routine and develop their business ideas, innovative products or services, scale an existing business idea and find new business opportunities, adapt their businesses to the new norms of the business environment with a focus on innovation. It promotes active learning in collaborative teams, where the learners and their business interests are at the center of the experimental and exploratory learning process.

Since 2020, the program has included students to foster experience and idea exchange between businesses and young specialists. Students participate in the workshops and work on tasks together with the teams, bringing fresh insights to the table. While these activities are not attached to an academic environment, high-level professionals from different fields join to facilitate and provide mentoring to participants. Importantly, the program does not offer formal tests or other forms of examination, instead it produces interactive content and a flexible learning environment, where the culture of failure and iterative trials are a significant part of the learning process. Importantly, the program sees participants as lifelong learners and the most important criteria for being a participant of SEB growth program is motivation and the business idea with the potential to be further developed throughout the program phases and beyond them. Although only the companies themselves can fully evaluate to what extent new principles of working are applied in their routines, it is possible to evaluate their change in turnover, new product launches and revenue stream.

Connected Learning Program, Vodafone Foundation

Presented by Rajnish Tiwari

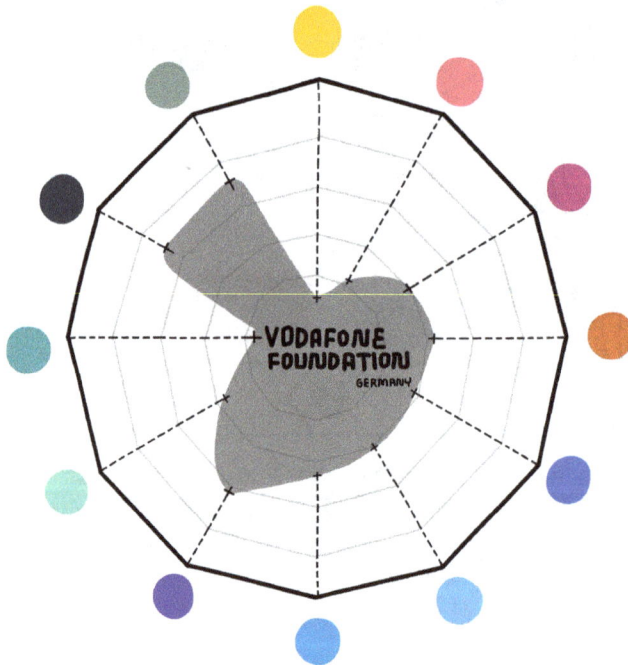

Vodafone Stiftung Deutschland (VFG) is a nonprofit corporate foundation in Berlin. It is a part of the international Vodafone Foundation Network. The foundation's goal is to reimagine education for the digital society. A critical concern is the new skills needed to actively shape the digital world and how new technologies can be employed to develop creative solutions to 21st-century societal challenges.

A part of VFG's work is dedicated to developing better understanding of how to create and exploit synergies between technologies and unique and irreplaceable human (cognitive) capabilities. Closely related to that is the question of how to explore new and promising ways for machines and humans to collaborate. It is, therefore, critical that learners and teachers not only dig deeper into the application part of a technology but also develop a thorough understanding of its fundamentals. In the words of Johanna Börsch-Supan, Director Strategy and Program at VFG "the ambition [is] to move that discourse from [merely] catching up to actually getting into a much more active role of enabling each and every one of us to be creators, and to be those who actually shape these technologies actively."

One of the programs initiated by VFG aims to foster "connected learning." Under this flagship program it launched a scheme called Digital Skills Europe (DSE), with an outlay of €20 million to support digital skills and education in 13 European countries. The program is expected to benefit 16 million learners between 2021 and 2025, limiting and reducing fear of technology through a human-centered approach that on the one hand considers the capabilities of humans and on the other hand also looks at where they feel uncomfortable with technologies.

More concretely, the foundation has a math game, or programming tool, for teachers with which they can tell stories. It also has little microcontrollers with which they can build instruments. This reduces fears and uncertainty around technology as well as helps the use of technology in fields where people already have expertise and comfort.

With the younger generations, the foundation focuses on trying to see how they can make videos for sharing on social media platforms. But VFG tries to make them reflect on the process of putting together a video while sensitizing them against fake news and preparing them to take care that the content is not harmful.

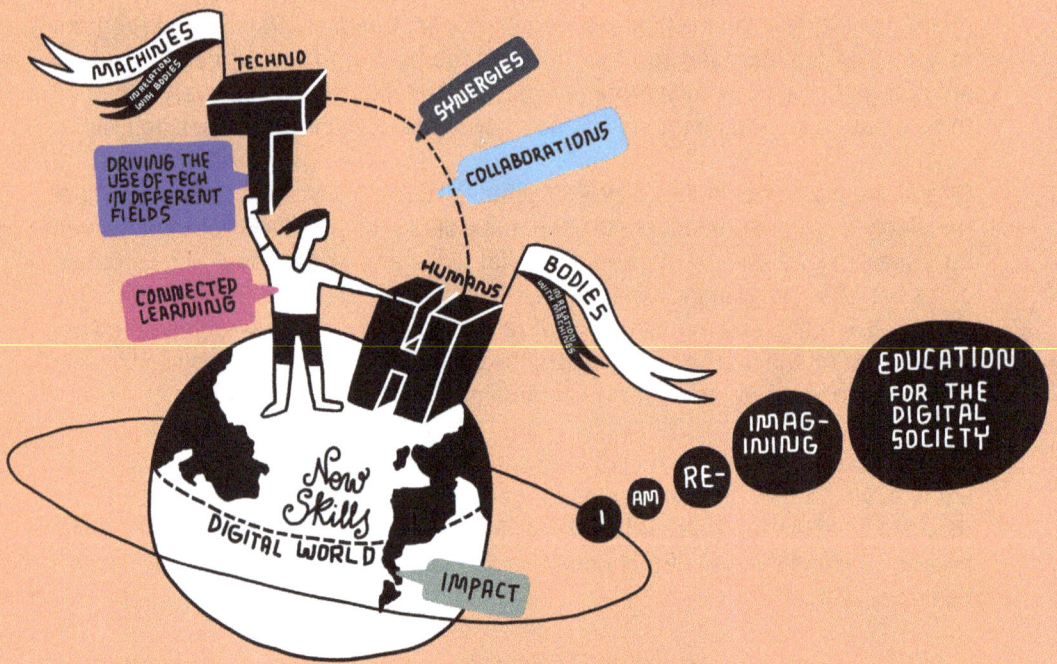

Digital Academy, TÜV NORD GROUP

Presented by Irina Fiegenbaum & Dietmar C. Schlößer

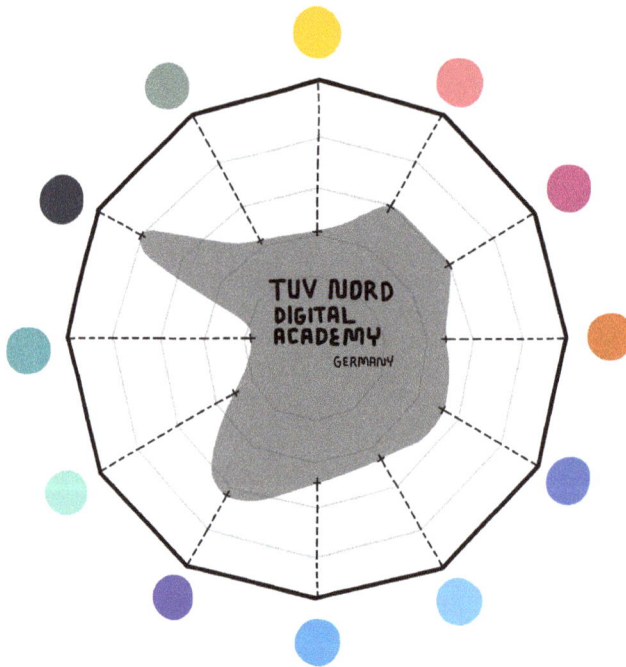

TÜV NORD's Digital Academy was initiated in 2017 to digitalize a 150-year-old traditional German-based company. The main feature of this digital enablement program is the digitalization from inside, acknowledging their employees as key success factors and the importance of upgrading their skills to be future proof for the new digital world. The initiative was created when TÜV NORD realized that the knowledge needed was company-specific and could not expect universities or external consultants to deliver this level of learning customization. Even TÜV NORD's educational business unit, called TÜV NORD Akademie, which is specialized in adult education and training, had never developed such a tailor-made and comprehensive enablement program.

To master this unprecedented challenge, a cross-functional team supported by all business units was deployed. During the process of trying to create a learning program for its employees, TÜV NORD realized that while they could outsource the delivery of the identified education content, they wanted control of the curricula. In other words, they needed a curriculum that was tailored to TÜV NORD's ever-changing business needs. The creation of the Digital Academy eventually allowed the company to formulate its own curricula, changing other elements of its learning landscape in the way.

For example, the company started in the training spaces used for other schooling on their campus and then moved first outside to the co-working spaces to distance the learners as much as possible from their daily routine. Subsequently, they created their own learning spaces based on the identified needs for the program, and eventually moved the entire program to 100% online due to the pandemic. The knowledge is delivered in a challenge-based format, asking the students to work on their own project, which takes 50% of their learning time. The projects resulting from the training can potentially become innovations that the company would bring to market or even new businesses, which is why the importance of the project element is extremely high.

It is important to note that the students in the program are employees, some very young, joining the company right after their graduation, while others have decades of experience. These are called digital experts (DE). Important outcomes from the training are the skills acquired, which can be applied directly during day-to-day work, as well as the innovative projects mentioned above, which are pitched at the end of the programme to a jury consisting of the company executive board in order to get support for further implementation. Moreover, an important outcome is a community that each digital expert can join. This community helps maintain the skills in the years to come and stay in touch with other "graduates." Another important outcome is new career perspectives: many of the digital experts received new tasks in their daily job, some of them got new positions more connected to digitalization and innovation; a few even gained an attractive promotion.

Originally, trainers were recruited from the consulting space to deliver the program, but the company later realized the need for deeper expert knowledge and therefore partnered with universities for theoretical content. For the online version of a program, in-company experts could contribute as well by creating and delivering the content.

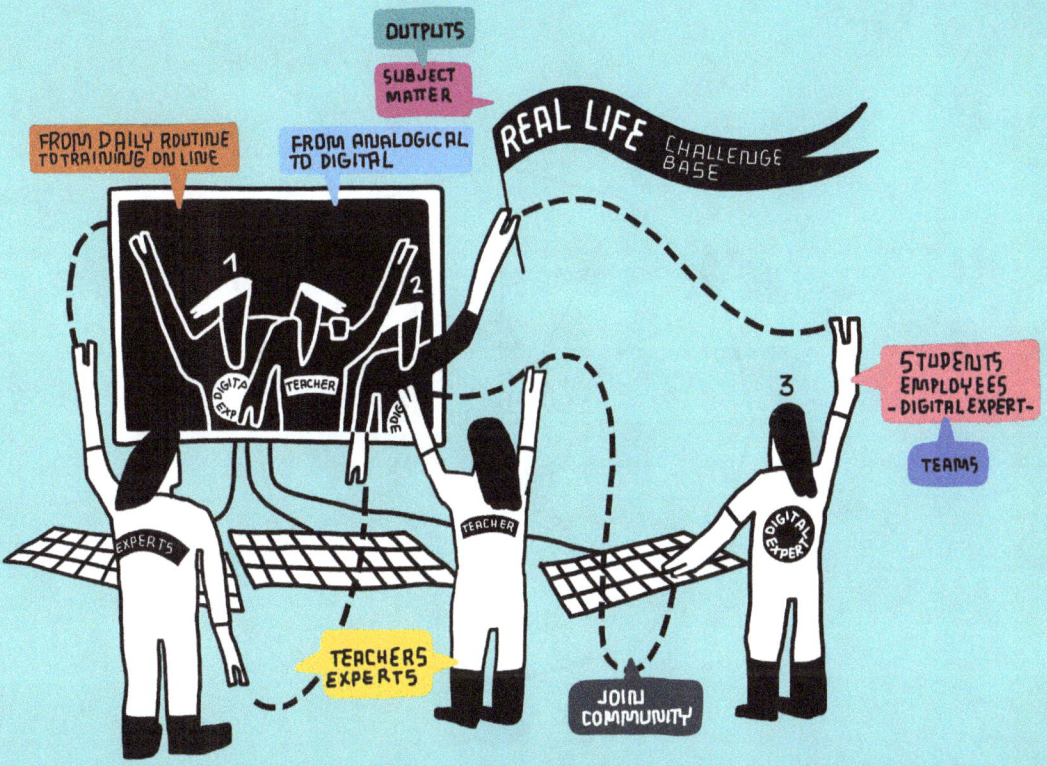

The College of Extraordinary Experiences
Presented by Kyriaki Papageorgiou

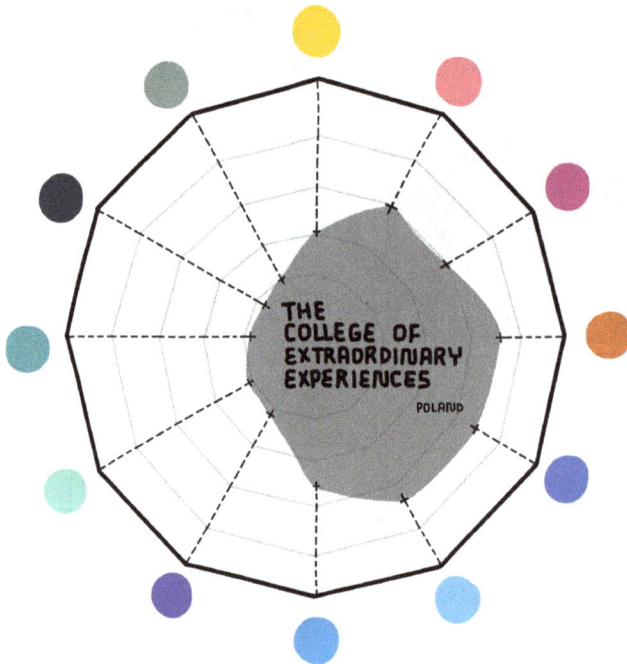

The College of Extraordinary Experience (COEE) offers an intense learning experience once a year for five days in a very unusual setting: a 13th-century castle in Poland. The origin of this college is traced back to 1998, when two business consultants wrote a piece on the "Experience Economy" in the *Harvard Business Review*.[103] They subsequently published a book with the same name the following year in which they further developed the core idea on which the College of Extraordinary Experience is built: that scripting and staging compelling experiences offers unique value, similar to commodities, goods and services. Approximately a decade later, additional publications on experience design institutionalized the field, as well as the art and science of designing unique learning experiences.

One of the key motivations of the COEE co-founders was to find new and better ways to connect people to learn from each other and innovate than in normal conferences. Having some experience with live action role-play events, they came up with the idea of bringing together professionals from different industries and backgrounds in a one-of-a-kind immersive setting: the Czocha Castle in Poland. There, participants put on capes and partake in several loosely structured activities that stimulate the circulation of ideas. As one participant has put it "it's like Hogwarts meets Disneyland, thoroughly spiced with Burning Man ethos and costuming."[104]

The methodology used in COEE is based on three principles: (1) co-creation, (2) flexible focus and (3) rapid prototyping. Co-creation is encouraged through the lively interactions between participants and the sharing of ideas that stem from their different professional, cultural and educational backgrounds. Flexible focus is learned by zooming in and out between the big picture and the tiny details. Lastly, rapid prototyping is emphasized through constantly reiterating the initial ideas through testing and feedback.

Another COEE participant[105] describes one concrete example of a challenge given to her team to tackle during her participation in COEE: their graduation performance. Once they took up the "hero's journey" idea by one of her teammates, they employed the steps used in storytelling and mythology to design the different trials that would take place around the castle. They designed elements such as "goblins" and "magic potions." Team members agreed to play the roles of certain mythical creatures that the heroes encountered along the way.

Additional testimonials attest to the singularity of the whole experience, the valuable lessons learned about innovation and the strong bonds built between participants. As one of the co-founders explained to us, the formula for creating memorable experiences involves first and foremost positive emotions and then artifacts, like a graduation hat or a prize, something material that can help people remember. The role of learning experience designers is one of stage designers, curators and guides.

EDTECH – FUTURE OF EDUCATION

Tech Futures Lab
Presented by Olga Kokshagina

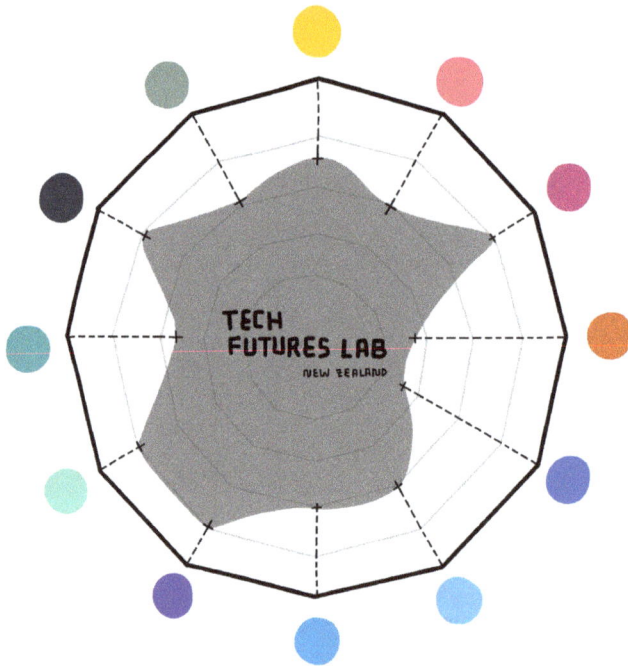

Established by education futurist Frances Valintine, Tech Futures Lab is New Zealand's only privately-owned graduate school. It is specifically designed to prepare people and organizations for the future of work. The educators are practitioners and thought leaders in disruption, innovation and the future of work. Their master of Technological Futures is designed to allow students to adapt to the demands of a rapidly changing world at any stage of their career. The students are expected to build on one of the emerging disruptive technologies such as AI, machine learning, blockchain, as well as non-digital tech, like human-centered design, to solve a problem or seize an opportunity.

The master's degree is project-based, practical and focused on giving learners the knowledge, the tools and the connections to succeed in the world outside the classroom and prepare them for the future. The program also aims to prepare future graduates to deal with societal shifts: influences from society that impact business such as circular, sharing and collaborative economies, the digital-first generation and the value of genuine indigenous perspectives and wisdom. The main focus is on future-oriented skills including critical thinking skills and tangible project experience to stay relevant and thrive in the face of inevitable change. Other skills that the program focuses on are applied skills that encourage innovative and creative thinking – like design sprints, agile methods and systems-led strategies.

Although the format is relatively traditional, with a 12- or 18-month master's degree including an online only option if needed, the Tech Futures Lab has certain unique characteristics designed to inspire people to refocus or future-proof their career, experience new things or guide them onto a completely new career path. More specifically, students are pushed to think of potential "visions of Aotearoa"[106] with the goal to honor te Tiriti o Waitangi and the rights of indigenous people in the constitution, the institutions and in everything the country does. Students and staff attending the programs are guided on "tikanga," Māori methodology and the Te Tiriti o Waitangi, acting as a bridge between Māori and Pākehā cultures, mindsets and values.[107]

Each semester contains immersion, project and assessment phases, presented in detail in the handbook.[108] Assessments are a combination of summative and formative assessments where formative assessments are designed to receive feedback from their peers and advisors with no grades and summative assessments are traditional academic assessments. Every student has a dedicated advisor to support and guide them throughout the duration of the program and connect them with other experts from industry or academia, to help round-out the research and project outcomes.

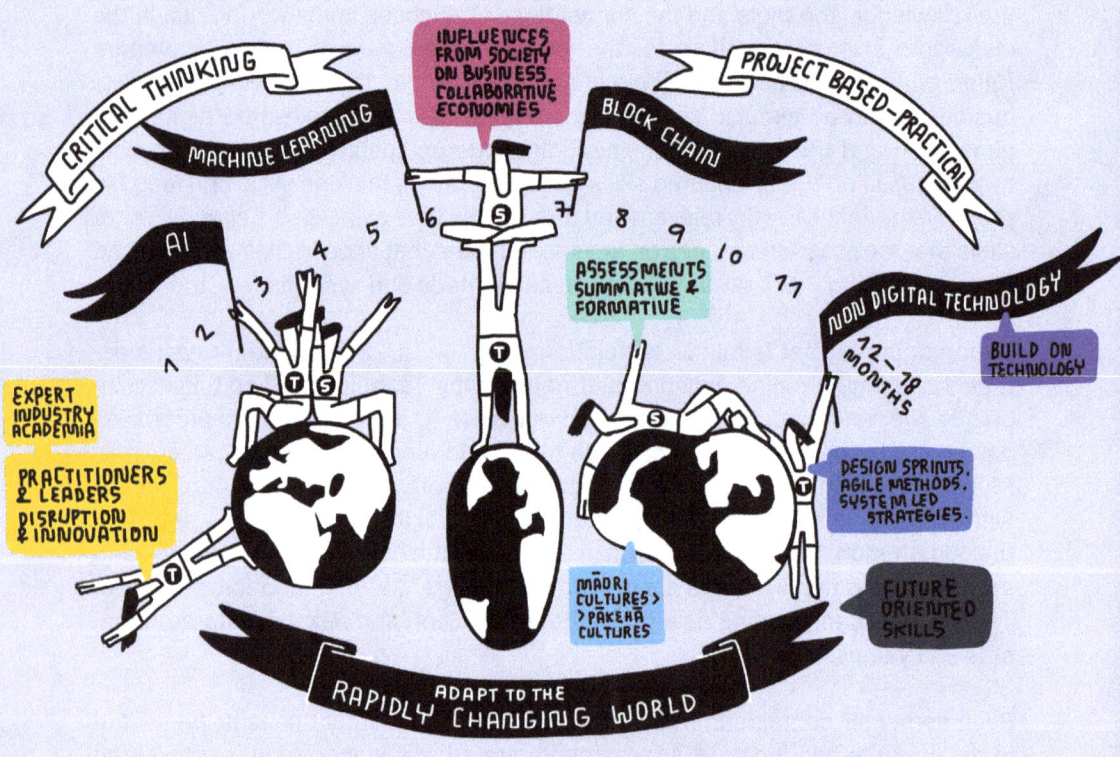

School of Humanity & Aweacademy

Presented by Olga Kokshagina

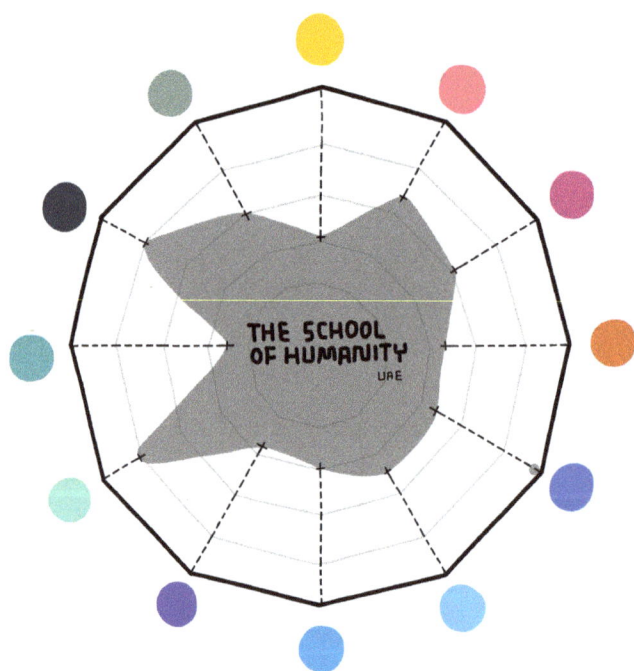

The School of Humanity was founded by Raya Bidshahri in 2021 to develop the skills and mindsets required to accelerate human progress and Aweacademy in 2017 as an online platform to "inspire a sense of awe and wonder in learners."[109]

Aweacademy is a project focused on preparing learners, educators and industry leaders for different futures. As indicated on the website, "Our vision is to bring a sense of awe and wonder into education, encourage learners to take a cosmic perspective, and have a species-wide positive impact." These two projects are complementary. The School of Humanity was created to reinvent what, how, why and where learning happens. According to Bidhahri, educational spaces must be transformed and adjusted to the reality we are living in. "The exciting innovations in the education space are happening at the '"edges"' of our education system – with the rise of new alternative school models."[110]

Learning is organized in sprints that last for six weeks. Every six weeks, learners embark on an interdisciplinary learning path of their choice. There are career paths like impact investing or data analyst; skill paths such as systems thinking and change, and self-knowledge and well-being; or challenge paths like food security or future of money. Throughout each path, learners participate in workshops, mentorship sessions, and active learning experiences including debate clubs and game nights helping them to acquire transferable skills. Instead of exams, learning outcomes are regularly evaluated through meaningful assessments including focus on competencies and a combination of project-based and personal evaluations are in place. The learning is interdisciplinary and customized to the learner's preferences.

The learning occurs online but the school is experimenting with physical spaces in several locations where learners can use facilities of co-learning spaces around the world and be able to receive the educators support face-to-face as well as engage with other learners.

Learning pace is also flexible and can be delivered as a full-time program, an extracurricular activity, or summer schools. Many learners are high school students who are looking for alternatives to supplement existing formal education.

BYJU'S
Presented by Rajnish Tiwari

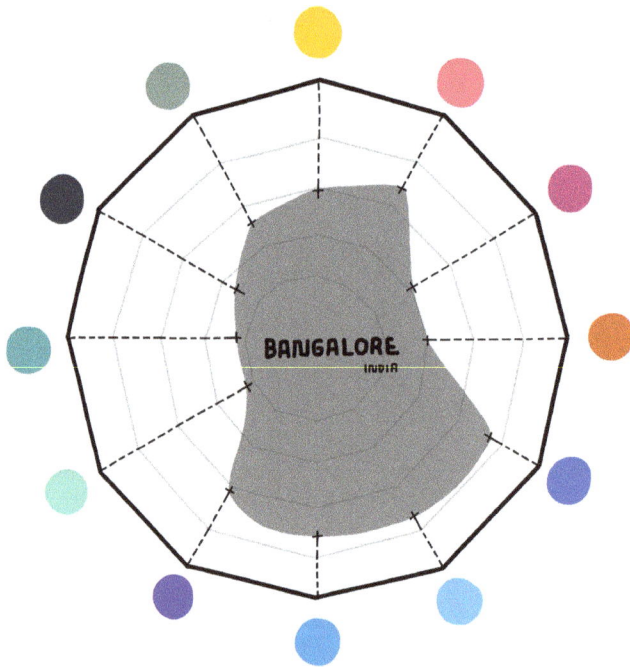

Byju's is an EdTech company headquartered in Bangalore, India. The company was founded in 2011 and has reportedly become the highest value EdTech company in the world, with an estimated market valuation of more than $40 billion, as of August 2021. Byju's offers online preparatory and tuition services in the form of smartphone apps on a freemium basis to students at all levels. The company is estimated to generate around $1 billion in revenues through global operations, 30% of which would come from the US market. Buoyed by the long months of Corona-induced lockdown, Byju's had reached a subscriber base of more than 80 million users, out of which nearly 5.5 million were paid subscribers.

Byju's grew in India by offering mobile phone-based online tuition services that in many cases could also compensate for lack of quality education in many schools. Especially in the semi-urban and rural areas, this connected pupils to highly qualified teachers and subject-matter experts living in other parts of the country. A Bloomberg report from 2018 says, "the app proved popular in a country where good teachers are scarce and methodologies antiquated and where many people first access the web by phone."[111]

Byju's has actively targeted gamification of education. Byju Raveendran, the co-founder, was quoted saying, "I want to Disney-fy education in India. [...] I want to do for education what Walt Disney did for entertainment. I want to make it engaging and fun, not just for the Indian kids but kids everywhere." Besides providing anytime, anywhere access to teaching material, tutors on the Byju's app also tackle complex subjects with storytelling, using real-life objects. The app features a mix of video, animation and interactive tools in order to bring clarity to complex subjects such as geometry, scientific experiments or history. About half of Byju's nearly 1,150-strong workforce (in 2018) is young filmmakers, musicians, graphic designers and animation experts, and the company employs two in-house bands to score background music. Each student can track their own progress and their learning is personalized through collaboration between content, media and tech teams.

Recently the company has acquired overseas firms and, thus, has created a global footprint. For example, in July 2021, Byju's acquired Great Learning for $600 million, an American upskilling platform that specializes in online higher education, offering certified courses in subjects such as data science and business analytics, AI and machine learning, cyber security and digital marketing. Courses at Great Learning are offered in collaboration with some of the world's highly renowned universities, such as MIT, Stanford, Northwest and the University of Texas.

Bakpax & Imbellus
Presented by Olga Kokshagina

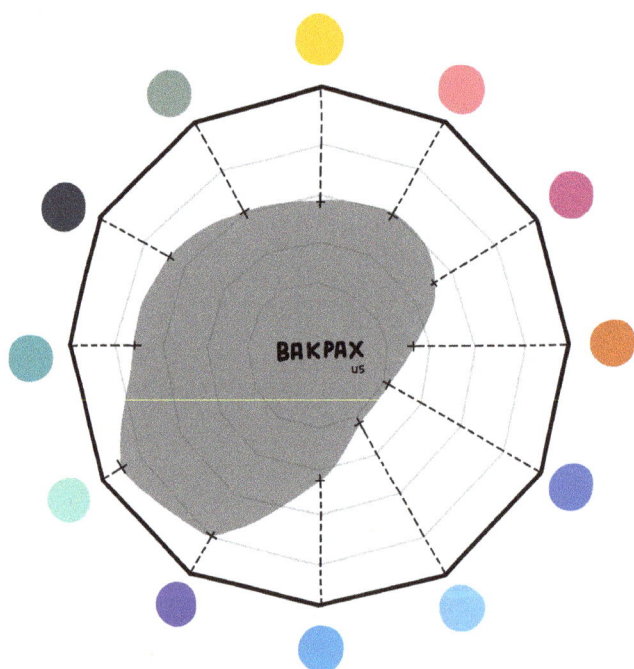

Established in 2017, Bakpax tackles one of the major pain points for teachers – evaluation. As indicated on the *Owl Website*,[112] BakPax is creating a platform that will be the hub of daily activity for a teacher. The goal is to leverage machine learning and AI to auto-grade student homework and provide daily actionable insights for teachers from this formative data. The real-time data will help teachers better tailor day-to-day instruction for their students.

Teachers can use the assignments already provided within the platform or add their own assignments. Students can complete their work online on any type of device or upload a document or photo. As indicated on the Bakpax website, the platform reads students' handwritten and typed submissions and grades assignments in seconds. Bakpax uses AI to read handwriting and grade assignments. It saves time for teachers while helping them create content and grading, provides students with instant feedback and gives you deeper insights into class performance. Teachers have the flexibility to rely on the platform only, or manually grade some of the assignments.

Students get instant feedback and teachers can save time in grading the assignments that represent 10–20 hours of their week on average. This simplifies creating and grading formative assessments but remains limited when it comes to reflective assessments, essays, etc. They provide solutions for free to both teachers and students with a premium package directly sold to schools and districts, rather than teachers.

Bakpax is a solution that solves a specific pain point for teachers. Looking forward, it would be great to see how the platform can be integrated with other online learning environments and allow for grading more subjective assignments. In that regard, another EdTech start-up – Imbellus[113] – attempts to build simulation-based cognitive assessments to evaluate 21st-century skills like problem solving, systems thinking and decision making. Imbellus studies these skills in action with employer partners and then brings that understanding to the education space for use in high-stakes standardized tests.

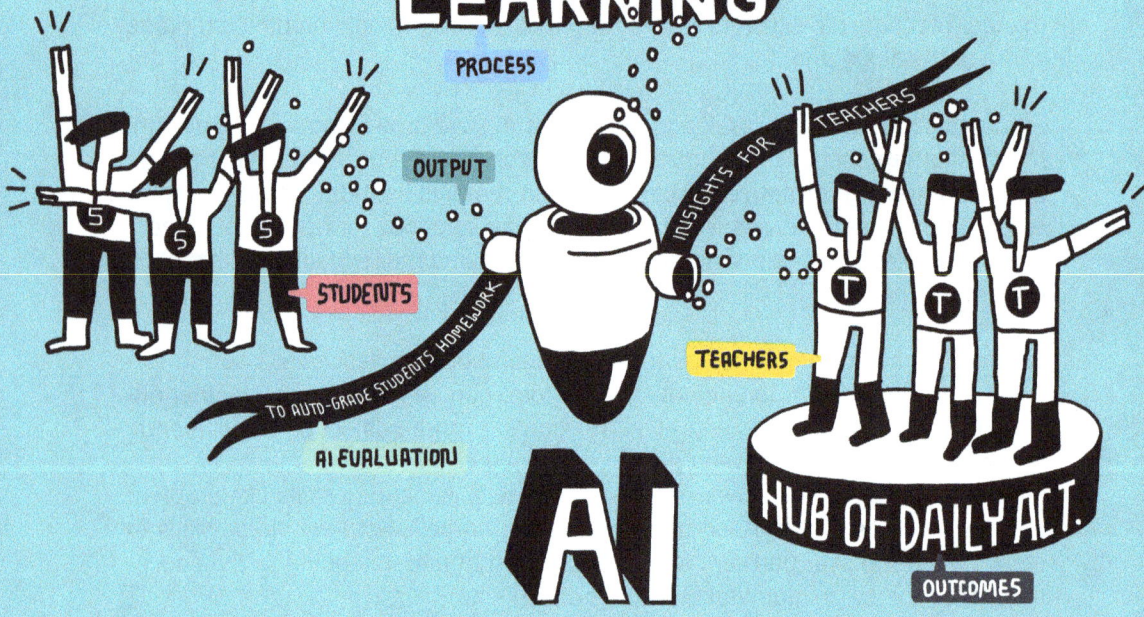

Classe Investigation – CLEMI

Presented by Olga Kokshagina

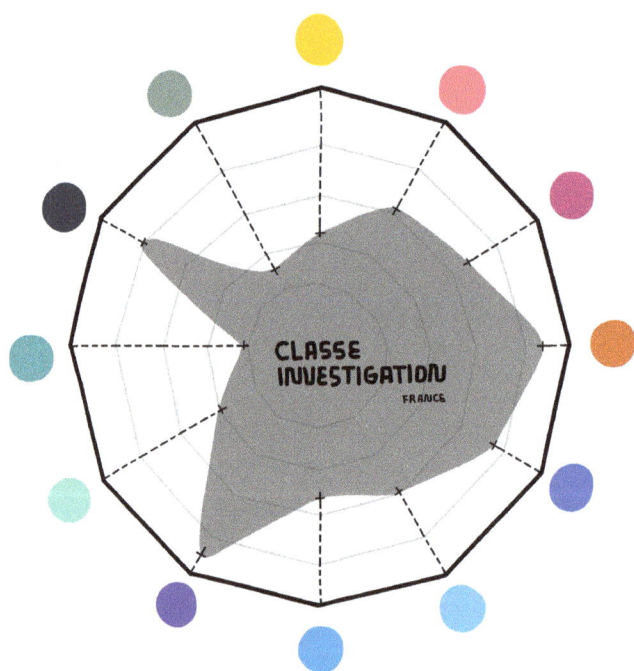

Serious games are games designed for purposes other than entertainment. Many examples exist in education. For example, Bogart Technologies is a serious game developed to enable accountants to become aware and comply with the restructured international Code of Ethics for Professional Accountants (Code), released by the International Ethics Standards Board for Accountants (IESBA) on the 9th of April 2018 in Australia.[114] Innovative Dutch[115] developed an innovation management game to help you run an innovation department. The game can be used for academic simulation, teamwork and personal development. Another example that is described in detail here is Classe Investigation developed by CLEMI.

CLEMI, part of Canopé Network (Réseau Canopé), overseeing Media and Information Literacy (MIL) in the French education system. CLEMI was created in 1983 with the mission to train teachers to a better knowledge of the news media system and to build children's citizenship skills by providing tools and fostering their critical thinking of media and information. Media literacy is a crucial asset to achieve a better understanding of the world.[116]

Classe investigation is an education game developed by CLEMI in collaboration with the MediaLab working group, made up of teachers and journalists. The goal of the game is to help learners understand what good quality journalistic investigation is. To achieve this goal, the game has developed two scenarios: "zoo alert" and "factory explosion." In groups of two, the students must transcribe the testimonies and clues they discover via text, audio and video, in order to ultimately produce journalistic content (print or digital format). The goal is to use different scenarios to explore how journalistic consent should be produced. Students explore how information should be structured, how to choose relevant sources, what their responsibilities are as journalists and finally what different professional constraints do they need to consider. At the end of the game, they can compare their work with that of a professional journalist: Mathilde Dehimi, reporter for France Inter. The learners can discover the constraints of the journalist's profession and understand how information is produced.

The format is relatively short and each game lasts for about 150 minutes with an additional feedback session. To help teachers use this game, a training module is developed for teachers to guide them. The feedback from teachers seems very positive: "Thank you for presenting us a tool that we will be able to easily reintroduce in our classes and for allowing us to be actors in our training by putting ourselves in the shoes of the students" (source: Clemi website).

The game is available to any public institution and resources are provided to teachers willing to incorporate it into their curriculum.

PART III

CREATING A FUTURE-READY LEARNING LANDSCAPE

There is a plethora of toolkits proposed by a variety of organizations that offer concrete activities to help embed creativity, innovation and entrepreneurship (CIE) for different purposes. Some of the most comprehensive collections of these employ design thinking as the central approach around which they position several specific tools or methods. For example, *Stanford d-school's Design Thinking Bootleg*[117] succinctly describes the five "process modes" involved in the innovation process: empathize, define, ideate, prototype, test. Subsequently, this presents several practical tools, like "How might we" questions, interviewing, brainstorming and testing with users. Similarly, Nesta's *Development Impact & You (DIY)* toolkit[118] is an easy-to-use guide aimed at practitioners working in the field of development that highlights approximately 30 tools organized into eight "wants." More concretely, if a practitioner wants to generate new ideas, *DIY* gives suggestions like "Thinking Hats" or organizing creative workshops. It also provides concrete worksheets, instructions, and examples of real-life situations where these were applied before.

Similar compendiums are offered by (just to name a few): *Radical Innovation playbook by Kokshagina & Alexander*,[119] *The perfect innovation toolkit* by the Board of Innovators,[120] *Fast track impact planning tool developed by Prof. Mark Reed and colleagues*,[121] the Great Teaching toolkit[122] and many EU-funded projects that resulted in developing toolkits and resources to support CIE activities. For example, LifeComp proposed the European Framework for Personal, Social and Learning to Learn Key Competence. The authors argue that LifeComp can be used as a basis for the development of curricula and learning activities fostering personal and social development, and learning to learn.[123] Another example is the EntreComp framework which aims to foster entrepreneurial capacity of European citizens.[124] One of the most recent frameworks proposed by the EU is HEI Initiative: Innovation Capacity Building for Higher Education – a new initiative to unlock the full innovation potential of higher education institutions' (HEIs) by increasing their entrepreneurial and innovation capacity whilst integrating them into Europe's largest innovation ecosystem.[125] (It is not a hyperbole to say that the majority of projects or institutions working in the fields of CIE have or aspire to have their own toolkit.)

These toolkits are a helpful resource to educators working in the areas of CIE, they help to think through the changes needed, structure the activities in the courses, identify the competences and capabilities that the CIE teaching should focus on and how spaces should be considered. Though, most of them are not designed with the learning activities and education in mind but designated to innovation practitioners. Therefore, they might be limited to consider the broader learning landscape within which they are applied. Subsequently, the majority of the critical learning elements identified in this book are neglected, alongside the imperative to change them. As our study has demonstrated, learning for CIE pushes against the traditional educational environment, challenging them through and through, from the role of the teachers and students to the expected outcomes and their evaluation. Our focus here is to help you consider how you are positioned against the 12 elements of the learning landscape (see Part I), to determine the current shape of your learning landscape and consequently design new learning experiences that will help you ride the waves of change.

In this section we outline some actions you might consider to purposefully ascertain where you currently stand and where you would like to go. We suggest four (non-linear) steps to take.

This is not a linear process and there is no one size fits all model. Your learning landscape is specific to your own broader environment. Therefore, our goal is to help you reflect on and analyze your current learning landscape, identify areas for improvement and design and test the most promising solutions. Different toolkits outlined above and resources captured in the Table presented in the Annex are to help you identify resources that work for you.

Understand Your Educational Environment

The 12 elements we identify and group under pillars of learning, learning journey and learning outcomes, are fundamental to any type of learning activity (see Part I). Therefore, a critical first step is to understand the extent to which your organization or the activities you coordinate have already started changing. What are the elements where transitions are well underway and which ones appear not to have changed at all?

By building on the examples presented in Part II, you can use the Figure on pages 170-171 to assess where your organization is positioned, from traditional to future ready. The closest to the inner circle you are, the more your characteristics follow the "status quo" or the educational protocols established in the past century. If you consider that certain elements have already shifted toward the future, position these closer to the outer circle accordingly. You can always do this exercise with different stakeholders within and outside of the organization to collect as many opinions as possible and then use the average of all the opinions to analyze where you are positioned, or disaggregate the data based on the type of stakeholders.

Once you have drawn your own "spider web" you are able to see more clearly where you stand and the type of elements that have been successfully shifted and how. Subsequently, you begin to think more critically whether this is enough or further improvements are needed. It is imperative to reflect on the elements that did not change for a while and grapple with the reasons why. Is it because they function properly or because they remain unnoticed?

UNDERSTAND YOUR EDUCATIONAL ENVIRONMENT

THINK ABOUT THE SHIFTS IN YOUR EDUCATIONAL ENVIRONMENT

USE SPIDER WEB TO INDICATE HOW YOUR ORGANIZATION IS POSITIONED ACROSS EACH SHIFT. POSITION YOUR SCORES ACROSS THE SPIDER WEB.

CREATE YOUR LEARNING LANDSCAPE

CONNECT THE SCORES ACROSS THE SPIDER WEB TO DRAW YOUR LEARNING LANDSCAPE.

CHALLENGE YOUR UNDERSTANDING

PRESENT THE SPIDER WEB TO OTHER STAKEHOLDER WITHIN AND OUTSIDE OF YOUR ORGANIZATION TO COLLECT THEIR FEEDBACK AND SEE HOW THEY WOULD POSITION THE SHIFTS THAT ARE CURRENTLY OCURRING IN YOUR LEARNING ENVIRONMENT.

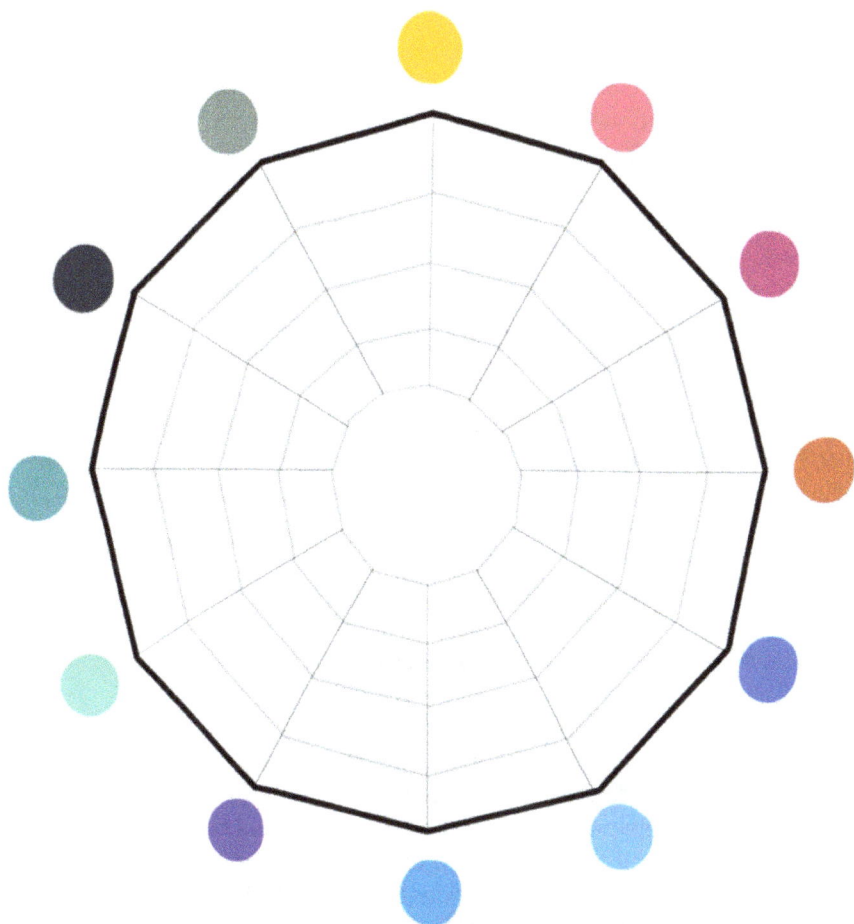

PILARS OF LEARNING

- 🟡 TEACHER
- 🔴 STUDENT
- 🔴 SUBJECT MATTER
- 🟠 SPACE

LEARNING JOURNEY

- 🔵 STYLE
- 🔵 PROCESS
- 🔵 PHYSICAL MATERIAL ARTIFACTS
- 🟣 DIGITAL TECHNOLOGY

LEARNING RESULTS

- 🟢 EVALUATION
- 🟢 OUTPUTS
- ⚫ OUTCOMES
- 🟢 IMPACT

Select the Elements to Focus on

Better understanding the broader environment within which your work is situated, especially the infrastructural limitations or institutional structures that might resist change, will enable you to better ascertain the kinds of elements that make most sense for you to intervene on. It can be that you feel that there are too many elements that require your attention or that you are positioned against a system that is simply too difficult to change. What is more, it can be the case that there are no resources, financial or otherwise, to support you. Whatever your specific circumstances might be, there are actions you can take nevertheless, or small changes you can introduce in your own work. Therefore, it is important to prioritize the areas you would like to focus on, recognizing that most elements are interconnected.

For example, if you decide to focus on processes and would like to design a learning journey that is more iterative and dynamic, then it is likely that you will also have to adjust how learners are evaluated (i.e., changing from summative to formative assessment forms; embedded self-assessments, peer feedback). As creative, innovative, or entrepreneurial efforts involve high uncertainty, risk and failing along the way, traditional evaluations that usually give a percentage of the grade to a mid-term exam would need to be replaced with other ways of assessing and communicating to the students how they are performing.

Selecting the elements to focus on prompts you to identify your priority elements and invites you to think about why the organization should focus on them. What is the internal and external evidence that the elements need to change? To what extent do you control these elements and what are the resources needed to achieve the desired changes? Here it is important to collect evidence on how these elements are currently operating and that they need to change. This evidence can be based on students' feedback in the case of formats and evaluation or issues with technological infrastructure, enrollment numbers and learners' appreciation of the content. At the same time, you need to look at the external signals: what are the general trends in learning, particularly in your own discipline? How do other institutions within and outside of your domain approach these shifts? These insights will help you to make a more informed decision on what to focus on initially.

You can start with any specific shifts or understand what type of shifts might be valuable for your specific institutions. Subsequently, determine four additional elements that you believe support these priorities. Taken together, these seven pieces will be critical in reshaping your learning landscape.

EXPLAIN YOUR CHOICES

o

EVIDENCE FOR CHANGE

COLLECT THE EVIDENCE THAT THE CHANGE IS NEEDED.

o

Reshape Your Learning Landscape

Once you narrow down your focus and have a good understanding of your elements, current condition or shape, start thinking of the concrete activities you would like to launch, as well as the resources you need, to help you successfully achieve the desired shifts. Resources might include new staff to assist you with the organization or delivery of your course, or new methods to make your learning journey process more iterative, exploratory and experimental. We recommend that you consider at least three actions for each of your main shifts, while always reflecting how these connect to the other relevant elements you have selected.

For example, if you decided to experiment with subject matter, and would like to introduce problem-based and challenge-based learning (CBL), the UN SDG goals are especially helpful. Here you need to be mindful of how exactly you present real-life societal challenges to your students and the precise deliverables you ask at the end of the course so that the learning journey lends itself to potentially valuable outcomes. Although most challenge-based learning initiatives do not go beyond the classroom, their potential for broader impact is enhanced if the latter is more deliberately thought through in the course design process.

Have you thought of co-designing the challenge with an industry partner, for instance? Inviting an industry partner not just at the end to select the best idea but engaging them through an entire project where students work on the subject that can lead to potentially important results for the industry and society. Here you need to carefully design not just the content and the assignments for the challenges but also pathways to impact. You can think of it as discovery, exploration and preparing a take-off approach when it comes to developing innovation.[126] Preparing the take-off or acceleration phase will help you think about how to help different stakeholders further develop these ideas outside of the learning experience and potentially bring learners to be part of the implementation journey. Once you have identified the concepts of CBL you would like to explore, then you need to test them from the learner's perspective, infrastructure, pedagogy, etc. Here you can use the principles of validated learning and learn start-up to test your pilot. What is important here is to be able to reject ideas based on the evidence collected and assumptions formulated in the first place. There are a plethora of toolkits and approaches to help you define the assumptions, think about the way to test them and process learning.[127]

And in parallel, do not forget to consider how you will measure the success or failure of learning. What are more suitable forms to evaluate the CBL activities? How can you achieve better outcomes for learners and all the organizations involved?

RESHAPE YOUR LEARNING LANDSCAPE

SHIFT YOU ARE WORKING NOW:

III

i.e. DESIGN A LEARNING JOURNEY WITH SEVERAL PARTNERS INVOLVED

II

i.e. CO-DESIGN A CHALLENGE WITH AN INDUSTRY PARTNER

i.e. PARTNERSHIP AGREEMENT

i.e. INDUSTRY PARTNER IS READY TO PARTICIPATE AGAIN

RESHAPE YOUR LEARNING LANDSCAPE

EACH LEARNING LANDSCAPE IS UNIQUE AND YOU CAN EXPLORE HOW THE COMBINATION OF DIFFERENT SHIFTS CAN LEAD TO DIFFERENT VERSIONS OF THE LEARNING LANDSCAPE.
WE USED THE TANGRAM ANALOGY FOR THIS.

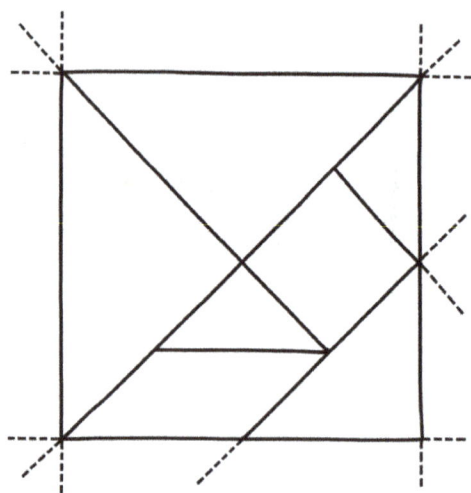

COLOR THE 7 PIECE WITH THE 7 MOST IMPORTANT SHIFTS

- TEACHER
- STUDENT
- SUBJECT MATTER
- SPACE
- STYLE
- PROCESS
- PHYSICAL MATERIAL ARTIFACTS
- DIGITAL TECHNOLOGY
- EVALUATION
- OUTPUTS
- OUTCOMES
- IMPACT

Reflect and Reiterate, or Shape-Shift Again!

It is important to remember that the entire process is iterative, and that you are dealing with high uncertainty. You need to be ready to change the course of action based on your testing, feedback and evidence collected along the way.

Systematically collecting and analyzing the reflections of all the actors involved in your course, from students and teachers to other peers across and outside the organization, is key for revising your initial assumptions and planning your next steps. As indicated earlier, all the elements of your learning landscapes are highly interconnected and you will soon realize that when you shift at least one element, you need to reconsider all the others and how the learning experience will look. At this point it would be important to ask: what else do you need to work on for the changes you introduced to work within the learning ecosystem? You might consider changing focus and choose different elements or pieces of the learning landscape to redesign and explore. Even if you focus on one or two shifts, you need to consider here how the changes you are integrating will be connected to other parts of the learning landscape; and how will you ensure that value is embedded, and the learning landscape is balanced again. Unless you are starting from scratch or have an abundance of resources at your disposal, we recommend not to try to tackle all the 12 elements at once, as this will likely generate mess and frustration.

One of the major elements to deal with here is communication and alignment. When additional elements need to change, you need to carefully think who the stakeholders are to bring on board, how to align across different priorities and make sure that the learning landscape is balanced and reflects the key changes made. For example, if you are planning to conduct CBL online, you need to make sure that all students are properly equipped to participate, that you are not leaving anyone out and that you are able to collect feedback on the engagement to potentially improve the way the challenge is designed and conducted. If you are planning to engage with industry, what type of residential intensive can you think of online or face-to-face? The residentials can be partly online for weekly feedback combined with an intensive week-end experience where industry and students work together or be focused on a student's placement within a company.

Once again, take stock of where you stand, re-select the elements you would like to focus on to create equilibrium and continue riding the wave of change!

REFLECT
REITERATE
OR SHAPE-SHIFT AGAIN

FOR EACH SHIFT, SUMMARIZE YOUR MAJOR LEARNINGS BELOW

EVIDENCE THAT THE SHIFT WORKS

_____
_____
_____

UNEXPECTED LEARNING SURPRISES

_____
_____
_____

HOW CAN YOU IMPROVE THE IMPLEMENTATION

_____
_____
_____

CONNECTIONS TO OTHER SHIFTS

_____
_____
_____

Below we provide examples of activities and resources that can be used for each shift.

Table 4. Examples of resources and activities for your learning landscape

Element	Future-ready learning landscape	Activities or actions	Resources
Pillars of learning			
Teacher	Various roles: coach, mentor, facilitator, curator, practitioner, learning designer; continuous upskilling	Take the self-paced course, designed for educators and school leaders to learn strategies to support students' creativity, communication, critical thinking and collaboration skills Use toolkits available to help you consider how to improve your teaching	https://edex.adobe. com/profession-al-learning/self-paced-course/teach-creativity-with-adobe-and-khan-academy https://www.greatteach-ing.com/resources
Student	Student at the center and directly in touch with the subject studied; creator of information	Students are accountable for their own teaching; active in collaborating with teachers to design their learning journey Students can train the growth mindset; reflect on their learning jour-ney by using different learning principles (think it through, make and use associations) Use reflective journals to document progress Facilitate study groups, think-pair-share strategies Flipped classrooms can be used to trans-form learning environ-ment in more active, dynamic space	The growth mindset playbook: https://trainugly.com/mindset/ More on reflective journals: https://wikieducator.org/Reflective_journals Bergmann, J., & Sams, A. (2012). Flip your classroom: Reach every student in every class every day. International society for technology in education.

Subject matter	Problem-based or challenge-driven	Introduce a challenge in your course around the SDGs, try to identify partners to help you organize the challenge and support the translation of the results; embed the challenge as a recurrent work and not a one-time initiative	SDGs Challenge-based learning Experiential learning Crowdsourcing; open innovation Responsible social innovation Open curriculum UN resources for SDGs
Space	Flexible spaces and the real world	Think of how you can leverage existing workplaces for more interactive experience: does the layout support collaboration? Is there a possibility to transform the place for more interactive activities? You can ask students and try to change the space in collaboration with them Design activities outside of the classrooms where students can visit organizations outside, work in collaboration with external entities during visits, internships and having industry in the class as well	New learning spaces, learning commons: https://www.educause.edu/research-and-publications/books/educating-net-generation/learning-spaces Kolb, A. Y., & Kolb, D. A. (2005). Learning styles and learning spaces: Enhancing experiential learning in higher education. *Academy of Management Learning & Education*, 4 (2): 193–212.

Learning journey			
Style	Team-based and collaborative	Review any collaborative activities that are currently embedded within the curriculum – how effective they are? how can they be improved? Please refer to toolkits and activities that can potentially be integrated and think what their value is; talk to students and collect their feedback. You need a structured approach with well-designed tasks for collaboration	Bielaczyc, K., & Collins, A. (2009). Learning communities in class-rooms: A reconceptu-alization of educational practice. *Instructional Design Theories and Models*, 2: 269–291. https://evidence-forlearning.org.au/the-toolkits/the-teach-ing-and-learning-toolkit/all-approaches/collaborative-learning/
Process	Iterative, exploratory and experimental	Think of how more iterative and explora-tory practices can be embedded in different learning activities. This can be reflected in the content, learning styles and learning results. For example, trial and learning approaches can be part of the learning lab facilities. Design thinking, lean start-up, concept-knowledge methods can be used as part of the learning facilities Anticipation-Action-Reflection (AAR) can be integrated to help learners continuously improve their thinking and act intentionally and responsibly toward collective well-being	Anticipation-Action-Reflection cycle: https://www.oecd.org/education/2030-pro-ject/teaching-and-learn-ing/learning/aar-cycle/ The experiential learning Agile lean start-up Design thinking

Physical material	Arts and crafts	Multiple learning styles might benefit from a variety of tools to enhance learning experience. This is if you can integrate sketches, post-its, prototypes, games as part of the learning journey. How can they be used? for what purpose? Games, for example, allow for in-person training, collaboration with other players and instant feedback on the actions that the players take Learning by design provides a framework where learning are producers of knowledge as well	Playful experimentation: Lego serious games https://www.lego.com/en-us/seriousplay https://dreamadream.org/ https://newlearningonline.com/learning-by-design/
Digital technologies	Interactive	Technology plays an active role in learning. IT infrastructure that fully supports learning space functions and learning pedagogy online should be carefully sought through. Chatbots, virtual whiteboards, VR/AR, interactive collaboration spaces online like Gather help to integrate the collaborative learning environment and design immersive experiences	https://immersivevreducation.com/ https://immersiveeducation.org/ https://secondlife.com/destinations/learning

Learning results			
Outputs	Written material, physical prototypes and action	Learning outputs should reflect the learning-by-doing and experiential learning. You might consider introducing different canvases, testing frameworks and prototyping as part of the learning outputs. Students can use canvases to come up with the ideas to solve specific challenges, to guide them to design tests and use a validated learning approach to validate their ideas before developing prototypes and iteratively test them again	Makerspaces/labs Validated learning approach Lean start-up, value proposition design, business model canvas https://edtechbooks.org/id/Prototyping_strategies
Outcomes	Personalized knowledge, skills, values, attitudes and meta-learning	Learning outcomes should reflect the knowledge or skills that will be most valuable to the student now and in the future. EU frameworks like help to guide the teachers on what skills, values, attitudes are important to embed in the learning practices. Furthemore, students need to reflect on their meta-learning. Systems thinking practices can be used. They can be used to adjust learning curricula	LifeComp (JRC) EntreComp (JRC) DigiComp Systems thinking

Impact	Societal	Impact of learning needs to be considered at the societal level where environmental factors need to be considered as well as the importance of culture and group aspects of learners. Different research impact canvases and toolkits can be useful to reflect on the impact of the education practices and adjust the learning practices to be more inclusive, collaborative and span beyond the classroom	Research for impact - canvas Fast track impact Impact planning toolkit Fast Track Impact – resources https://www.fasttrack-impact.com/resources RI toolkit https://esrc.ukri.org/re-search/impact-toolkit/ Tools for researchers: the research toolkit http://globalkidsonline.net/tools/ Research impact as ethos: https://cur.org.au/cms/wp-content/uploads/2020/09/rickards-et-al-2020-research-impact-as-ethos.pdf Foresight and futures literacy
Evaluation	Multidimensional	Use the HEInnovate EPIC tool template to assess "entrepreneurial mindset," as well as creative, collaborative and leadership competences	https://heinnovate.eu/sites/default/files/EPIC_user_guide.pdf https://learningfromexperience.com/assessments/

It is important to emphasize that the choice and combination of different tools and methods are unique to the setting and particular circumstances of individual organizations or learning communities. CIE learning initiatives that are addressing the current shifts can take various forms and shapes.

RIDING
THE WAVES
OF CHANGE

In this book, we aimed to capture the transitions in the learning landscape that are needed and propelled by creativity, innovation and entrepreneurship (CIE). Building on the insights and expertise of more than 136 stakeholders we interacted with in our interviews or workshops delivered in the context of the VISION project. Our interlocutors have helped us identify major changes, innovations required, advances and transitions that are currently underway – shifts. These shifts point to the ongoing transformation of higher education and pave the way for new learning experiences and collaborations across disciplines and sectors, while at the same time redirecting attention to the original purposes of the educational institutions. This book draws from the rich body of knowledge around CIE – extending the latter to the educational practices. To identify the shifts, we co-designed our visions from the perspectives of HEIs, industries, policy makers and EdTechs and explored how CIE can inform our thinking and approaches to tackling these.

The shifts identified are structured across three different areas. First, pillars of learning as foundational elements that serve as a basis of our educational systems. Second, the learning journey captures the way knowledge is structured and transmitted to different individuals and the infrastructure required to support this. Finally, learning results are crucial to evaluate and reflect on how effective the learning is for an individual, group and society at large.

Our goal is to inspire our readers to reflect on their learning or teaching environment, think about shifts they observe and what challenges or opportunities they see for the future of learning within their own context. Our snapshots into the future and prompts on how to start creating a future-ready learning landscape are to guide readers in transforming their own infrastructures and practices and ride the waves of change.

We are of course not exhaustive in our presentation of the shifts, and regard our suggestions of tools and cases as examples. One of the challenges we did not delve into in this book relates to finances and the changes that might be needed in the existing funding models of public and private universities. HEIs' business models are largely based on the principle that teachers teach, and students learn and the latter or the government pays. Some of the more recent online models based on MOOCs rely on similar concepts: content access by students and teachers preparing the content in advance. Yet, we all know that this must change. Indeed, researchers are interested in the business models of entrepreneurial university[128] or looking into potential ways of disruptive innovation can be an opportunity to make a quality higher education fundamentally affordable and thereby allow many more people access to its benefits.[129] What is clear is that to be entrepreneurial requires changes to the underlying value propositions, value creation and value capture

194

activities of a university, which comprises their business model. Funding models can be seen as a horizontal shift, and it is central to the successful changes in the learning landscape.

Going forward, when designing your new courses, training material on CIE or trying to improve the existing ones – try to think of what shifts you need to address first and how you can gradually bring the learning environment to the next level for your students. We hope the readers will build on these shifts, improve them and design their own approaches toward teaching CIE and organizing their learning environment.

AUTHOR BIOS

Kyriaki Papageorgiou

Kyriaki is the director of research at Fusion Point, Esade Business and Law School. Her work is located at the intersection of anthropology and STS. Her current research examines policies, discourses and practices of innovation in tackling big societal challenges, and the emergent role of robotics and AI in transforming work and daily lives. She is particularly interested in the future of learning and engaged in collaborative projects on co-creation in education and challenge-driven innovation.

Olga Kokshagina

Olga is an associate professor of innovation and entrepreneurship at the EDHEC Business School. She is a recipient of the vice chancellor research fellowship at the RMIT University, focusing her research in the areas of strategic management of design, open & radical innovation, entrepreneurship and the role of emerging technologies in transforming the nature of work. She is a member of the French Digital Council (CNNUM) and a co-author of a recently published book, *Radical Innovation Playbook*.

VISUAL THINKER

Irma Arribas

Irma is a PhD architect. Her work focuses on understanding architecture as a means of communication. Because of that, she works in the academic, artistic and research world, designing and producing spaces and atmospheres for learning, criticism and the emergence of knowledge. She is currently linked to European and Asian universities of art, architecture, design and entrepreneurship as well as museums and cultural centers around the world.

SNAPSHOTS OF THE CONTRIBUTORS

Rajnish Tiwari

Rajnish is a senior research fellow at the Institute for Technology and Innovation Management of Hamburg University of Technology (TUHH) in Germany, where he has been responsible for the VISION project. He leads the research program Global Innovation at TUHH and at the Hochschule Fresenius University of Applied Sciences. Rajnish focuses on digital transformation as an enabler of "affordable excellence" and has advised Germany's Federal Ministry of Education and Research concerning "new global innovation pathways."

Carina Leue-Bensch

Carina is a professor of Innovation Management and Corporate Entrepreneurship at the Faculty of Management, Worms University, Germany and an innovation manager at Lufthansa Systems. She graduated in Business Informatics as well as Technology and Innovation Management (MSc) and holds a PhD in Innovation Management from University of Potsdam, where she is still engaged as an associated researcher at Hasso-Plattner-Institute. Her main research interests are (Corporate) Entrepreneurship & Innovation, University-Industry collaboration and new ways of delivering education.

Beata Lavrinoviča

Beata is a project manager at Social Innovation Centre with experience in social innovation, social entrepreneurship, education sciences, civic participation, gamification and youth work R&I. She is experienced in service design and cross-sectoral project development and promotes social innovation internationally. She holds academic degrees in Business Administration and Intercultural Relations and is a PhD student of Educational Sciences. Her research interests lay in innovation in education, transdisciplinary learning and transversal skills development among youth.

Dietmar C. Schlößer

Dietmar is responsible for Digitalization & Innovation at TÜV NORD GROUP. His mission is to drive the digital transformation and innovation management of the whole group. Dietmar is very enthusiastic about his role as catalyst of forward-looking technology with the focus on helping TÜV NORD GROUP succeed in the phygital age. Before joining TÜV NORD GROUP, he served as CIO at Compu-Group Medical and Deloitte.

Irina Fiegenbaum

Irina is a senior manager for Digitalisation & Innovation at TÜV NORD GROUP. She is engaged in digital transformation initiatives of the company, with a focus on developing training approaches for enabling employees. She is passionate about innovation and drives establishment of innovation management structures in the company. She has received her Dr. Sc in Innovation Management from Lappeenranta University of Technology, with research and teaching focus on open innovation and strategic entrepreneurship.

VISION
PROJECT
PARTNERS

Partners	Project partner description
University EMUNI PROJECT COORDINATOR	Since its establishment in 2008, Euro-Mediterranean University (EMUNI) has become an international institution gathering expert knowledge and experience of the Euro-Mediterranean countries and thus contributing to the creation of an integrated Euro-Mediterranean HEI and research area. It has more than 130 members from 33 countries (EU, Middle East and North Africa) and a network of 150 different HEIs and research institutions. Its aim is to bridge the North and the South Mediterranean with an emphasis on raising awareness about the EU and raise the quality of higher education through the implementation of study and research programs.
ispim CONNECTING INNOVATION PROFESSIONALS	ISPIM - International Society for Professional Innovation Management is a network of researchers, industrialists, consultants and public bodies who share an interest in innovation management. Founded in 1983 by Professor Knut Holt in Norway, ISPIM is the oldest, largest and most active innovation association in Europe.
FUTURE AGENDA	Future Agenda is a global open think tank and advisory firm that helps organizations to explore the key issues, challenges and opportunities for the next decade and develop and launch innovative new businesses, products and services. Working in collaboration with corporate, academic and government partners around the world, it brings together experts to debate the core changes and shares meaningful insights on the pivotal emerging shifts and acts on the implications. www.futureagenda.org
SOCIĀLĀS INOVĀCIJAS CENTRS SIC www.socialinnovation.lv	The Social Innovation Centre (SIC) provides non-formal learning about social innovation, social entrepreneurship, political processes and policy formation for disadvantaged society groups, integration and increase of society participation in social and political processes. The main goal is to promote the idea and movement of social innovation and entrepreneurship as a strategic tool for sustainable development.
stim NOW EVERYONE CAN CREATE	STIM is a start-up consultancy – spin off of Mines ParisTech in France (https://www.wearestim.com/). STIM builds on the most advanced research on innovation management and innovative design to spread to the world the very best scientific methods for innovation. STIM is recognized by the French government as a jeune entreprise innovante (J.E.I.) and is eligible to Crédit d'impôt recherche (C.I.R). STIM provides consultancy and training services to the MNCs based in the internal R&D or collaboration with the research centers. Since 2014 STIM has developed a team of 25 experts skilled in innovation and entrepreneurship (engineers and PhDs).

TUHH Hamburg University of Technology	TUHH is a competitive university that acts sustainably, sets itself high performance and quality standards and aims for excellence in basic research and in areas of expertise. Approximately 100 professors and another 700 scientific staff members at 80 institutes and scientific workgroups are responsible for the education of almost 8,000 students, 20 percent of whom come from abroad. TUHH cooperates extensively with business and industry around the world. These partners include both leading global corporations and small and midrange businesses, and they are the backbone of the development of successful cooperation networks. The exchange and transfer of technology and knowledge with industrial partners has always been a core element of TUHH's activities.
esade	ESADE ranks among the top 10 business schools in Europe in the most important International MBA, Executive Education and university program polls. The institution's main objective is to train individuals to be highly competent professionals, fully conscious of their social responsibility. ESADE is a founding member of the Community of European Management Schools (CEMS), the most prestigious European network on the university level. ESADE was one of the first business schools to obtain the three most recognized awards in the sector: International AACSB, EQUIS and AMBA. ESADE has pioneered research in creativity and learning, innovation, open innovation in the public sector, entrepreneurial skills and management practices.
six	SIX (Social Innovation Exchange) has been building the global field and movement of social innovation for the last 10 years. SIX is a social innovation exchange built on mutual value, relationships and knowledge. SIX works globally to facilitate purposeful cross-sector conversations, that challenge and inspire people to use innovation to increase social impact. https://socialinnovationexchange.org/
innofora	Innofora provides organizations with director-level thinking and expertise to solve their innovation priorities, and training and events based on cutting-edge, evidence-based innovation management research and insight. Areas of focus include Setting and Changing Innovation Culture, Ideation and Creative Problem Solving, Opportunity Identification and Evaluation, and Strategic Planning. Innofora is an SME. innofora.eu
TÜV NORD	Since its foundation 150 years ago, the TÜV NORD GROUP (TNG) has been a global technical service provider, which deals in safety and trust. Experts and specialists of TNG have been testing machinery, equipment and products, auditing quality management systems in Germany and abroad. With more than 10,000 employees, the Group offers a wide range of innovative services in testing, certification, engineering, consulting and training.

per ceptos	Perceptos is a start-up and spin-off of the Technical University Munich whose core competency is the digital transformation of collaboration processes for innovation. More precisely, Perceptos transformed workshop collaborations methodologies (e.g., brainstorming, business model generation workshops, retrospective meetings) for the usage in an online platform. Currently the main activities of Perceptos reside in the development and provisioning of their web application IdeaClouds (www.ideaclouds.net) and in the facilitation of digital workshops using this web application if requested by organizations.
DE G DE GRUYTER	Headquartered in Berlin, De Gruyter is an independent scholarly publisher with a history dating back more than 260 years. De Gruyter has a strong international presence with additional offices in Basel, Beijing, Boston, Munich, Vienna and Warsaw. In total, De Gruyter publishes 900 journals and 1,300 new book titles every year as well as 40 digital products across 28 different subject areas. De Gruyter has an annual turnover of 65 million euros and has 350 employees worldwide.
Lufthansa Systems	Lufthansa Systems is an information technology service provider for the aviation industry. It has around 2,200 employees in several locations in Germany and offices in 16 other countries. The company is headquartered in Raunheim near Frankfurt. The company's portfolio includes consulting, development and implementation of customized industry solutions as well as the operation of applications in the company's own data centers.
RMIT UNIVERSITY	RMIT University, officially the Royal Melbourne Institute of Technology (RMIT), is a public research university in Melbourne, Australia. RMIT is a multi-sector university of technology, design and enterprise. RMIT's mission is to help shape the world through research, innovation and quality teaching. With strong industry connections forged over 133 years, collaboration with industry remains integral to RMIT's leadership in education, applied research and the development of highly skilled, globally focused graduates.

PEOPLE WHO SHARED WITH US THEIR VISION OF THE FUTURE OF LEARNING[130]

N	Name	Affiliation	Position
1	Adam El Rafey	10 year old change advocate	Public Speaker
2	Agnis Stībe	EM Normandie Business School	Director Artificial Intelligence
3	Ana Silveira	Associação Kokoro	Manager
4	Andre Renz	Weizenbaum Institut	Researcher
5	Anton Graschopf	Austrian Council for Research and Technology Development	Science Policy Advisor
6	Aravind Chinchure	QLEAP Academy	Founder & CEO
7	Ben Eubanks	Lighthouse Research & Advisory	HR industry analyst and influencer
8	Bert F. Hölscher	ARKADIA Management Consultants	Partner, Digital Transformation Expert
9	Bert-Ola Bergstrand	Social Capital Forum	Chairman and co-founder at Social Capital Forum
10	Bruce Hecht	VG2Play	CEO/CTO
11	Carlos Jimenez Härtel	Science|Business	Chairman of the Board
12	Chad Lubelsky	The J.W. McConnell Family Foundation	Acting Chief Program Officer
13	Christiana Gardikioti	Meraki People	Founder and Team Leader
14	Christine Preuschl	Hochschule für Musik und Theater	Project coordinator Innovative Hochschule: Stage_2.0
15	Charles Swoboda	Marquette University	Innovator-in-residence
16	Clare Stead	Oliiki Limited	CEO
17	Claudio Feijoo	Technical University of Madrid	VP for Entrepreneurship
18	Claus Raasted	Extraordinary College	Founder
19	Cristina Armuña	RuleEleven and BusinessADN	RuleEleven / BusinessADN
20	Dan Sleeman	RMIT Activator	Head of product and education

21	Danica Purg	IEDC-Bled School of Management	President
22	David Porter	Commonwealth of Learning	(former) Senior higher education adviser
23	Diana Bernal	Planet Pilots	Co-founder
24	Esther Wojcicki	Singularity University	Professor
25	Emma Kiraly	Junior Achievement Europe	Senior Program Manager
26	Enrico Poli	Zanichelli Venture	Director
27	Fahad Bubshait	Nuat VR	CEO
28	Felise Maennig-Fortmann	Konrad Adenauer Foundation	Advisor Education Policy
29	Finn Macken	Minerva / Education project / Thread	Student / Partnerships Executive / Researcher
30	Fyodor Ovchinnikov	Evolutionary Futures Lab	Co-Founder & Director
31	Florian Fiedler	Blockbay GmbH	CEO & Co-Founder
32	Francis Petersen	University of the Free State	Vice Chancellor
33	Frank Piller	RWTH Aachen University	Professor
34	Gerhard Reitschuler	Austrian Council for Research and Technology Development	Officer for Macroeconomic Development and Trends
35	Giuseppe Provenzano	Union for the Mediterranean Secretariat	Advisor for Research and Innovation
36	Goran Lazarevic	Hochschule für Musik und Theater	Project-coordinator for Hamburg Open Online University (HOOU)
37	Hannes Aichmayr	EdTech Austria	Managing Director
38	Jaan Aps	Stories For Impact	CEO and Senior Consultant
39	Javier Fernandez	Spanish Ministry of Education	Education Advisor
40	Johanna Börsch-Supan	Vodafone Foundation Germany	Director Strategy and Program

41	Johanna Maaghul	ODEM SA	Chief Operating Officer/Lead Strategist
42	John Bessant	University of Exeter	Professor
43	John Moravec	Education Futures	Researcher, futurist, author, knowmad
44	John Wood	Leadership and collective growth	Leadership Solutions Global
45	Juste Rakštyte Hoimian	Lithuanian Innovation Centre	Project Manager
46	Kalevi Ekman	DFGN - Aalto University	Professor
47	Karla Taboada	Domitila technologies	CEO & Founder
48	Kaymin Martin-Burnett	Minerva	Student
49	Kelly Fawcett	Foundation of Young Australians	Research + Policy Lead
50	Lars Lin Villebaek	Educatefor.Life Planet Kids	CEO
51	Lisa Andrews	Singularity Australia	CEO
52	Lou Aronica	The Fiction Studio	Writer, editor, publisher
53	Louise Pulford	SIX	CEO
54	Lucia Die Gil	Greaterthan Enspiral Foundation	Partner Director
55	Manjula Mishra	Pathrise - Professional Training & Coaching	Researcher | Data Scientist
56	Marc Fuster Rabella	OECD Centre for Educational Research and Innovation	Education Policy Analyst
57	Margherita Bacigalupo	European Commission Joint Research Centre	Scientific Officer
58	Marielza Oliveira	UNESCO/EDUCATION 2030	Director China Office
59	Martin Rademacher	German Rectors' Conference	Project Lead "Hochschulforum Digitalisierung"
60	Matthias Hillner	Glasgow school of art in Singapore	Programs director

61	Matthias Kaiserswerth	Hasler Foundation	Managing Director
62	Maximilian Räthel	Volkswagen Foundation	Program Director
63	Mohammed El Razzaz	Union for the Mediterranean Secretariat	Regional Coordination Coordinator
64	Moonsup Kim	Minerva	Student
65	Mónica Bello	CERN	Curator and Head of Arts at CERN
66	Naveed A. Malik	Virtual University of Pakistan	Founding Rector
67	Nada Trunk Širca	University of Primorska, ISSBS and EMUNI	Professor and researcher
68	Nelson Inno	weSpark - Innovation Agency	Founder & CEO
69	Oliver Janoschka	Hochschulforum Digitalisierung (Stifterverband)	Managing Director
70	Paco Ramos	Turning Tables	UX product manager
71	Pablo Garcia Tello	CERN	Section Head of the Development of EU Projects & Initiatives
72	Peter Hesseldahl	Mandag Morgen	Editor and journalist
73	Philipp Brunner	Industriewissenschaftliches Institut – IWI (Vienna, Austria)	Deputy Managing Director, Head of Innovation & Networks
74	Ponmalar N. Alagappar	Centre for Initiative Talent and Industrial Training, University of Malaya	Deputy Director of Industrial Training
75	Prema KV	MIT Bengaluru, Manipal Academy of Higher Education (MAHE), India	Professor & Head, Department of Computer Science & Engineering
76	Quim Sabria	EdPuzzle	Founder
77	Raya Bidshahri	School of Humanity	Founder & CEO
78	Richard Maaghul	ODEM SA.	Chief Executive Officer
79	Richard Robinson	Guanghua MBA Program, Peking University	Clinical Professor of Entrepreneurship
80	Rita G. Klapper	Manchester Metropolitan University	Reader in Enterprise and Sustainability

81	Robert Ransick	MCAD	Vice President of Academic Affairs for Minneapolis College of Art and Design
82	Ronny Röwert	Hamburg University of Technology	Project coordinator digital.learning.lab
83	Sahar Albaharna	Impactique	Innovation Coach and CEO
84	Sanda Gertnere	Ghetto Games	Co-founder
85	Sandra Otto	Future of work collective	Co-founder
86	Sanjaya Mishra	Commonwealth of Learning	Education Specialist, eLearning
87	Sara Roversi	Future Food institute	President
88	Smriti Pahwa	MOC Mindset	Founder Senior Consultant
89	Stéphan Vincent-Lancrin	OECD Centre for Educational Research and Innovation	Deputy Head of Division and Senior Analyst
90	Susan Basterfield	Greaterthan	Partner
91	Susann Roth	Asian Development Bank (ADB)	Chief of Knowledge Advisory Services Center
92	Teresa Franqueira	Design Factory Aveiro	Coordinator of Design Factory Aveiro
93	Thomas Ravenscroft	The Skills Builder Partnership	Founder and CEO
94	Tina Ladwig	Hamburg University of Technology	Specialist for the strategic development of Teaching and Learning in Digital Times
95	Uros Sikimic	3DLateral	Head of business development
96	Valerij Dermol	DERMOL Digital Business Solutions	Professor and researcher
97	Valtencir M. Mendes, PhD	UNESCO/EDUCATION 2030	Global Education Coalition - Global nonprofit Lead
98	Vera Martinho	JA Europe	Director for Education and Impact
99	Waldo Soto	Ashoka/2811	Ashoka Consultant, Co-founder of 2811
100	Zane Vītola	SEB bank	Innovation Centre Manager

NOTES

1. Erasmus + Knowledge Alliance Project Number: 612537-EPP-1-2019-1-SI-EPPKA2-KA. https://www.vision-project.org/

2. In addition to the book authors, the following were involved in the collection of empirical material through interviews: Rajnish Tiwari (TUHH), Beata Lavrinoviča (Social Innovation Centre), Louise Pulford (SIX), Jerneja Penca, MItja Erževič, Ana Šajn and Hamid Abdel-Zpheiry (EMUNI).

3. Edwards-Schachter, M., García-Granero, A., Sánchez-Barrioluengo, M., Quesada-Pineda, H., & Amara, N. (2015). Disentangling competences: Interrelationships on creativity, innovation and entrepreneurship. *Thinking Skills and Creativity*, 16: 27–39; Ferland, L. W. (1988). The underlying relationship between creativity, innovation and entrepreneurship. *The Journal of Creative Behavior*, 22(3): 196–202.

4. Young, J. G. (1985). What is creativity? *The Journal of Creative Behavior*, 19(2): 77–87.

5. Amabile, T. (2011). *Componential Theory of Creativity* (pp. 538–559). Boston, MA: Harvard Business School.

6. Bledow, R., Frese, M., Anderson, N., Erez, M., & Farr, J. (2009). A dialectic perspective on innovation: Conflicting demands, multiple pathways, and ambidexterity. *Industrial and Organizational Psychology*, 2(3): 305–337.

7. Lewrick, M., Omar, M., Raeside, R., & Sailer, K. (2010). Education for entrepreneurship and innovation: "Management capabilities for sustainable growth and success" *World Journal of Entrepreneurship, Management and Sustainable Development*; Shane, S. (2012). Reflections on the 2010 AMR decade award: Delivering on the promise of entrepreneurship as a field of research. *Academy of Management Review*, 37(1): 10–20.

8. Crossan, M. M., & Apaydin, M. (2010). A multi-dimensional framework of organizational innovation: A systematic review of the literature. *Journal of Management Studies*, 47(6): 1154–1191.

9. Neck, H, Neck C., & Murray, K. (2021). *Entrepreneurship: The Practice and the Mindset*.

10. Vesper, K. (1982). Introduction and summary of entrepreneurship research. In C. Kent, D. Sexton, & K. Vesper (eds.), *Encyclopedia of Entrepreneurship* (pp. xxxi–xxxviii). Englewood Cliffs: Prentice-Hall.

11. Spence, N. A. (2020). *Designing for Epistemic Agency: How University Student Groups Create Knowledge and What Helps Them Do It* [The University of Sydney]. https://ses.library.usyd.edu.au/handle/2123/22348

12. Ibid., 4 quoting Damşa, Nerland & Andreadakis, 2019, 3.

13. Seifert, C., & Chapman, R. (2015, April 15). *The Coaching Transformation. Inside Higher Ed.* https://www.insidehighered.com/views/2015/04/27/essay-making-switch-professor-coach

14. Lund Dean, K., & Forray, J. M. (2020). Educators as curators: Displaying the caring art of teaching in management education. *Journal of Management Education*, 5: 527–532. https://doi.org/10.1177/1052562920945348

15. Morris, J., & Imms, W. (2019). Teacher as Practitioner (TAP) program helps keep teachers in the profession. EduResearch Matters. https://www.aare.edu.au/blog/?p=3676

16. Wagner, E. D. (2021). Becoming a learning designer – Design for learning. In J. K. McDonald & R. E. West (eds.), *Design for Learning: Principles, Processes, and Praxis*. EdTech Books. https://edtechbooks.org/id/learning_designer?book_nav=true

17. https://en.unesco.org/themes/education/sdgs/material

18. Bayley, J. E., & Phipps, D. (2019). Building the concept of research impact literacy. *Evidence & Policy: A Journal of Research, Debate and Practice*, 15: 597–606.

19. Blackmore, P., & Kandiko, C.B. (2011). Interdisciplinarity within an academic career. *Research in Post-Compulsory Education*, 16: 123–134; Bridle, H., Vrieling, A., Cardillo, M., Araya, Y., & Hinojosa, L. (2013). Preparing for an interdisciplinary future: A perspective from early-career researchers. *Futures*, 53: 22–32.

20. Rïdberg, K., Lundqvist, U., Malmqvist, J. & Hagvall Svensson, O. (2020). From CDIO to challenge-based learning experiences-expanding student learning as well as societal impact? *European Journal of Engineering Education*, 45(1): 22–37.

21. Mulgan, G., Townsley, O., & Price, A. (2016). The challenge-driven university: How real-life problems can fuel learning. *Nesta*.

22. Savery, J. R. (2015). Overview of problem-based learning: Definitions and distinctions. *Essential Readings in Problem-Based Learning: Exploring and Extending the Legacy of Howard S. Barrows*, 9: 5–15.

23. Gallagher, S. E., & Savage, T. (2020). Challenge-based learning in higher education: An exploratory literature review. *Teaching in Higher Education*: 1–23.

24. Mulgan, G., Townsley, O., & Price, A. (2016). The challenge-driven university: How real-life problems can fuel learning. *Nesta*.

25. OECD. (2017). *The OECD Handbook for Innovative Learning Environments Educational Research and Innovation*. Paris. doi: 10.1787/20769679

26. Kariippanon, K. E., et al. (2020). The 'why' and 'how' of flexible learning spaces: A complex adaptive systems analysis. *Journal of Educational Change*, 21(4): 569–593. doi: 10.1007/s10833-019-09364-0

27. ACTIU (2019) *The Future of Coworking and Flexible Spaces*. Available at: https://www.actiu.com/en/articles/news/the-future-of-coworking-and-flexible-spaces/ Accessed March 30, 2021.

28. McLaughlin, P. & Faulkner, J. (2012) Flexible spaces ... what students expect from university facilities, *Journal of Facilities Management*, 10(2): 140–149. doi: 10.1108/14725961211218776

29. Benade, L. (2019). Flexible Learning Spaces: Inclusive by Design?, *New Zealand Journal of Educational Studies*, 54(1): 53–68. doi: 10.1007/s40841-019-00127-2; Mulcahy, D., Cleveland, B. & Aberton, H. (2015). Learning spaces and pedagogic change: Envisioned, enacted and experienced. *Pedagogy, Culture and Society*, 23(4): 575–595. doi: 10.1080/14681366.2015.1055128

30. Kariippanon, K. E., et al. (2020). The 'why' and 'how' of flexible learning spaces: A complex adaptive systems analysis. *Journal of Educational Change*, 21(4): 569–593. doi: 10.1007/s10833-019-09364-0

31. Quote: Today "a classroom can be outside, in an elderly centre, in a church, in a company. There are many places where we can learn and teach" (Teresa Franqueira). Community spaces could become learning spaces for design thinking and ethnographic design.

32. Micheli, P., et al. (2019). Doing design thinking: Conceptual review, synthesis, and research agenda. *Journal of Product Innovation Management*, 36(2): 124–148. doi: 10.1111/jpim.12466

33. Marcus, G. E. (1995). Ethnography in/of the world system: The emergence of multi-sited ethnography. *Annual Review of Anthropology*, 24(1): 95–117. doi: 10.1146/annurev.an.24.100195.000523

34. https://www.tacitproject.org/peripatetic-learning

35. The Future of Learning and Teaching: Big Changes Ahead. An interview with Prof. Tricia McLaughlin https://www.rmit.edu.au/study-with-us/education/discover-education/the-future-of-learning-and-teaching-big-changes-ahead-for-education

36. Munge, B., Thomas, G., & Heck, D. (2018). Outdoor fieldwork in higher education: Learning from multidisciplinary experience. *Journal of Experiential Education*, 41(1): 39–53.

37. Blair, D. J. (2016). Experiential learning for teacher professional development at historic sites. *Journal of Experiential Education*, 39(2): 130–144.; Seaman, J., Brown, M., & Quay, J. (2017). The evolution of experiential learning theory: Tracing lines of research in the JEE. *Journal of Experiential Education*, 40(4): NP1–NP21.

38. Puckett, K. (2017). The future of education. https://www.the-possible.com/future-of-education-digital-campus-learning-teaching/

39. A. Almajed, V., Skinner, R., & Petersen, T. (2016). Winning collaborative learning: Students' perspectives on how learning happens. *Interdisciplinary Journal of Problem-Based Learning*, 10(2); Sawyer, R. K. (2015). A call to action: The challenges of creative teaching and learning. *Teachers College Record*, 117: 100303.

40. Hawlina, H., Gillespie, A., & Zittoun, T. (2017). Difficult differences: A socio-cultural analysis of how diversity can enable and inhibit creativity. *Journal of Creative Behaviour*, 53(2): 133–144.

41. Ibid.

42. Gardiner, P. (2020). Learning to think together: Creativity, interdisciplinary collaboration and epistemic control. *Thinking Skills and Creativity*, 38: 100749.

43. Ibid.

44. Rienties, B., Køhler Simonsen, H., & Herodotou, C. (2020, July). Defining the boundaries between artificial intelligence in education, computer-supported collaborative learning, educational data mining, and learning analytics: A need for coherence. In *Frontiers in Education*, 5: 128.

45. Jeong, H., Hmelo-Silver, C. E., & Yu, Y. (2014). An examination of CSCL methodological practices and the influence of theoretical frameworks 2005–2009. *International Journal of Computer-Support Collaborative Learning*, 9: 305–334. doi: 10.1007/s11412-014-9198-3

46. https://www.futurelearn.com/info/courses/differentiating-for-learning-stem/0/steps/99516 Accessed July 30, 2021.

47. Kolb, A. Y., & Kolb, D. A. (2005). Learning styles and learning spaces: Enhancing experiential learning in higher education. *Academy of Management Learning & Education*, 4(2): 193–212.

48. Kolb, A. Y., & Kolb, D. A. (2009). Experiential learning theory: A dynamic, holistic approach to management learning, education and development. *The SAGE Handbook of Management Learning, Education and Development*, 42: 68.

49. Kolb, D. (1984). *Experiential learning as the science of learning and development*. Englewood Cliffs, NJ: Prentice Hall.

50. Hatchuel, A., Le Masson, P., & Weil, B. (2017). CK theory: Modelling creative thinking and its impact on research. In *Creativity, Design Thinking and Interdisciplinarity* (pp. 169–183), Singapore: Springer.

51. https://spin.atomicobject.com/2017/05/19/design-thinking-supplies/

52. https://www.theconfidentteacher.com/2012/12/post-it-note-pedagogy-top-ten-tips-for-teaching-learning/

53. https://www.workshopper.com/post/design-thinking-phase-4-everything-you-need-to-know-about-prototyping#toc-sketches-and-diagrams

54. https://www.lego.com/en-us/seriousplay

55. Daid T. J. (2012). Exploring Play/Playfulness and Learning in the Adult and Higher Education Classroom. https://eric.ed.gov/?id=ED554701

56. Ibid.

57. https://trydesignlab.com/blog/bauhaus-school-five-lessons-for-todays-designers/

58. https://lab.cccb.org/en/lessons-from-the-bauhaus-for-the-21st-century/

59. https://europa.eu/new-european-bauhaus/index_en

60. Santoso, G. (2015). Technology as a driver of skills obsolescence and skills mismatch: Implications for the labour market, society and the economy. *ANU Undergraduate Research Journal, 7*: 49–62.

61. Schneider, S., & Kokshagina, O. (2020). Digital Technologies in the Workplace: A Ne(s) t of Paradoxes. ICIS; Schneider, S., & Kokshagina, O. (2021). Digital transformation: What we have learned (thus far) and what is next. *Creativity and Innovation Management.*

62. Personal interview, conducted on September 21, 2020.

63. Glen, R., Suciu, C. & Baughn, C. (2014). The need for design thinking in business schools. *Academy of Management Learning & Education, 13*(4): 653–667. doi: 10.5465/amle.2012.0308

64. Hatch, M. (2013). *The Maker Movement Manifesto: Rules for Innovation in the New World of Crafters, Hackers, and Tinkerers.* New York: McGraw-Hill Education, 11.

65. Cope, J., & Watts, G. (2000). Learning by doing: An exploration of experience, critical incidents and reflection in entrepreneurial learning. *International Journal of Entrepreneurial Behaviour & Research, 6*(3): 104–124; Noyes, E. (2018). Teaching entrepreneurial action through prototyping. *The Prototype-It Challenge Entrepreneurship Education and Pedagogy, 1*(1): 118–134.

66. Maker Ed. (n.d.). *The mission of Maker Ed is to harness the potential of making to transform teaching and learning.* Available at: https://makered.org/about/ Accessed March 30, 2021.

67. Martinez, S. (2019). *The Maker Movement: A Learning Revolution.* Available at: https://www.iste.org/explore/In-the-classroom/The-maker-movement%3A-A-learning-revolution Accessed March 30, 2021.

68. Blikstein, P. (2014). Digital defabrication and "making" in education: The democratization of Invention, in Walter-Hermrmann, J. and Büching, C. (eds.). *FabLabs: Of Machines, Makers and Inventors.* Bielefeld: De Gryter, Transcript (pp. 203–222). doi: 10.14361/transcript.9783839423820.203

69. Berglund, A. & Leifer, L. (2013). Why we prototype! An international comparison of the linkage between embedded knowledge and objective learning. *Engineering Education, 8*(1): 2–15. doi: 10.11120/ened.2013.00004

70. Colegrove, P. T. (2016). Makerspaces in libraries: Technology as catalyst for better learning, better teaching, in *UNESCO-UNIR ICT & Education Latam Congress 2016*, 133–141. Available at: http://research.unir.net/unesco-congreso/wp-content/uploads/sites/76/2016/06/u2016-COLEGROVEPatrick.pdf Accessed 30 March 2021.
Julian, K. D., & Parrott, D. J. (2017). Makerspaces in the library: Science in a student's hands. *Journal of Learning Spaces, 6*(2): 13–21.

71. Gershenfeld, N. (2012). How to make almost anything: The digital fabrication revolution. *Foreign Affairs, 91*(6): 43–57.

72. https://live.fablabs.io/

73. https://fablabserasmus.eu/

74. Diez, T. (2012). Personal fabrication: Fab labs as platforms for citizen-based innovation, from microcontrollers to cities, in *Digital Fabrication*. Basel: Springer Basel (pp. 457–468). doi: 10.1007/978-3-0348-0582-7_5

75. Chua, C.K., Leong, K.F., & Lim, C.S. (2003). *Rapid Prototyping Principles and Applications*. Singapore: World Scientific Publishing Co.

76. Richert, Anja, Mohammad Shehadeh, Lana Plumanns, Kerstin Groß, Katharina Schuster, & Sabina Jeschke. (2016). Educating engineers for industry 4.0: Virtual worlds and human-robot-teams: Empirical studies toward a New Educational Age, in *2016 IEEE Global Engineering Education Conference (EDUCON)*, 142–149. IEEE.

77. For example, Trilling, B., & Fadel, C. (2009). 21st century skills: Learning for life in our times. San Francisco: John Wiley & Sons; OECD. (2018). *The Future of Education and Skills. Education 2030*. Paris: OECD Publishing; *Council of the European Union. (2018). Council Recommendations of 22 May 2018 on Key Competences for Lifelong Learning*. Brussel: Council of the European Union.

78. Billett, Stephen. (2018). Distinguishing lifelong learning from lifelong education. *Journal of Adult Learning, Knowledge and Innovation, 2*(1): 1–7.

79. World Economic Forum. (2016). The future of jobs: Employment, skills and workforce strategy for the fourth industrial revolution. Global Challenge Insight Report.

80. Sleeman, D. (2019). Experiential learning, entrepreneurship and enterprise: Designing learning for the future of work, in *Transformations in Tertiary Education* (pp. 213–28). Springer.

81. Shrivastava, A. K., Rana, S., Mohapatra, A. K., & Ram, M. (2019). *Advances in Management Research: Innovation and Technology*. CRC Press.

82. Bansal, P., Bertels, S., Ewart, T., MacConnachie, P., & O'Brien, J. (2012). Bridging the research–practice gap. *The Academy of Management Perspectives*, 73.

83. Bayley, J. E., & Phipps, D. (2019). Building the concept of research impact literacy. Evidence & policy. *Journal of Research, Debate and Practice, 15*: 597–606; Rickards, L., Steele, W., Kokshagina, O., & Morales, O. (2020). Research Impact as Ethos. RMIT University, Melbourne. ISBN 978-1-922016-81-2. 27 pp.

84. H. Buijtendijk, & E. Eijgelaar. (2020). Understanding research impact manifestations in the environmental policy domain. Sustainable tourism research and the case of Dutch aviation. *Journal of Sustainable Tourism*: 1–18.

85. McKenzie, F., Sotarauta, M., Blažek, J., Beer, A., & Ayres, S. (2020). Towards research impact: Using place-based policy to develop new research methods for bridging the academic/policy divide Regional Studies. *Regional Science, 7*(1): 431–444.

86. Palincsar, A., DellaVecchia, G., & Easley, K. M. (2020). Teacher education and its effects on teaching and learning. In *Oxford Research Encyclopedia of Education*.

87. Kokshagina, O., Rickards, L., Steele, W., & Moraes, O. (2021). Futures Literacy for Research Impact in Universities. *Futures*.

88. Mulgan, G., Townsley, O., & Price, A. (2016). *The Challenge-Driven University: How Real-Life Problems Can Fuel Learning*. London: NESTA.

89. Bialik, M., Martin, J., Mayo, M., & Trilling, B. (2016). Evolving Assessments for a 21st Century Education. *Center for Curriculum Redesign.*

90. See, e.f. Mulgan, et al., 2016.

91. Fruchter, R., & Lewis, S. (2003). Mentoring models in support of P5BL in architecture/engineering/construction global teamwork. *International Journal of Engineering Education, 19*(5): 663–671.

92. McMaster University. (2021). About GRADE, viewed March 29 2021, https://cebgrade.mcmaster.ca/aboutgrade.html.

93. Marcus, 2020.

94. Fadel, C., & Center for Curriculum Redesign. (2015). *Redesigning the Curriculum for a 21st Century Education.* https://curriculumredesign.org/wp-content/uploads/CCR-FoundationalPaper-Updated-Jan2016.pdf

95. OECD. (2019). Attitudes and Values for 2030: Conceptual Learning Framework. *OECD Future of Education and Skills 2030.* www.oecd.org/education/2030-project/learning/attitudes-and-values

96. Björklund, T. A., Keipi, T., Celik, S., & Ekman, K. (2019). Learning across silos: Design Factories as hubs for co-creation. *European Journal of Education, 54*(4): 552–565. https://doi.org/10.1111/ejed.12372

97. Ibid. p. 556.

98. https://www.hs-fresenius.com/ Accessed July 2021.

99. https://www.mcad.edu/assessment/design-outcomes Accessed in August 2021.

100. https://www.futureofworkcollective.com/how

101. Quote from the interview with Sandra Otto – CEO of the Future of Work collective.

102. This snapshot was developed in collaboration with Irēna Vercmane, Innovation Lead at SEB bank Latvia.

103. Pine II, B. J., & Gilmore, J. H. (1998). Welcome to the experience economy. *Harvard Business Review.* https://hbr.org/1998/07/welcome-to-the-experience-economy

104. https://boingboing.net/2018/11/06/the-college-of-extraordinary-e.html

105. https://medium.com/@teodorasandu/at-the-college-of-extraordinary-experiences-you-live-in-a-castle-are-greeted-by-goblins-and-wear-d0dd06f0b5b9

106. Aotearoa is a Māori name. Māori, New Zealand's indigenous population, migrated from Polynesia around 1000 years ago. They comprise 16.5% of New Zealand's population.

107. https://thespinoff.co.nz/partner/tech-futures-lab/06-04-2021/back-to-the-future-how-returning-to-study-can-change-your-career-path/#.YHd-tUKgcAY.twitter Accessed July 20, 2021.

108. https://themindlab.com/app/uploads/sites/4/2021/07/public-facing-mtf-handbook-2022-g17-g18-v1-4-.pdf

109. https://inlandempire.us/riverside-city-college-received-1-67m-grant-for-stem-and-nursing-pathways/

110. https://humaneeducation.org/the-school-of-humanity-accelerating-human-progress-an-interview-with-raya-bidshahri/

111. Rai, S. (September 21, 2021). *Byju's Is Said to Accelerate IPO Plans as India Tech Booms*. Bloomberg. https://www.bloomberg.com/news/articles/2021-09-09/byju-s-is-said-to-accelerate-ipo-plans-as-india-tech-booms

112. https://owlvc.com/portfolio-bakpax.php

113. Recently Imbellus was acquired by a gaming company – Roblox to build a system for fair, objective and inclusive assessments.

114. https://www.cpdaccounting.com/learn/course/external/view/elearning/2/bogart-technologies

115. https://www.innovativedutch.com/innovation-management-game/

116. https://www.clemi.fr/fr/en.html

117. https://dschool.stanford.edu/resources-collections/browse-all-resources

118. https://diytoolkit.org/

119. Kokshagina, O., & Alexander, A. (2020). The radical innovation playbook. In *The Radical Innovation Playbook*. Berlin/Boston: De Gruyter.

120. https://www.boardofinnovation.com/guides/the-perfect-innovation-toolkit/

121. https://www.fasttrackimpact.com/resources

122. https://www.greatteaching.com/resources

123. Sala, A., Punie, Y., Garkov, V., & Cabrera Giraldez, M., LifeComp: The European Framework for Personal, Social and Learning to Learn Key Competence, EUR 30246 EN, Publications Office of the European Union, Luxembourg, 2020, ISBN 978-92-76-19417-0, doi: 10.2760/922681, JRC120911

124. Bacigalupo, M., Kampylis, P., Punie, Y. & Van Den Brande, L. EntreComp: The Entrepreneurship Competence Framework. EUR 27939 EN. Luxembourg (Luxembourg): Publications Office of the European Union; 2016. JRC101581.

125. https://heinnovate.eu/en

126. Kokshagina, O., & Alexander, A. (2020). The radical innovation playbook. In *The Radical Innovation Playbook*. Berlin/Boston: De Gruyter.

127. Just to name a few: Lean start-up approach; Evidence-based learning; Radical innovation toolkit exploration phase.

128. Posselt, T., Abdelkafi, N., Fischer, L., & Tangour, C. (2019). Opportunities and challenges of higher education institutions in Europe: An analysis from a business model perspective. *Higher Education Quarterly, 73*(1): 100–115. https://doi.org/10.1111/HEQU.12192; Abdelkafi, N., Hilbig, R., & Laudien, S. M. (2018). Business models of entrepreneurial universities in the area of vocational education – an exploratory analysis. *International Journal of Technology Management*, 77(1–3): 86–108. https://doi.org/10.1504/IJTM.2018.091716

129. Christensen, C. M., Horn, M. B., & Johnson, C. W. (2011). *Disrupting Class: How Disruptive Innovation Will Change the Way the World Learns (vol. 1)*. New York: McGraw-Hill.

130. Only those who gave their consent to be listed in our book are included here.

ISBN: 978-3-11-069759-9
e-ISBN (PDF): 978-3-11-075220-5

https://doi.org/10.1515/9783110752205

Despite careful production of our books, sometimes mistakes happen. Unfortunately, a wrong EU funding logo was included on page 4 in the original publication. This has been corrected. We apologize for the mistake.

Library of Congress Control Number: 2021941764

**Bibliographic information published
by the Deutsche Nationalbibliothek**
The Deutsche Nationalbibliothek lists this publication in the Deutsche Nationalbibliografie; detailed bibliographic data are available on the internet at http://dnb.dnb.de.

The book is published open access at www.degruyter.com.

Cover image and illustrations
Irma Arribas Perez

Typesetting
Irene Sierra

Printing and Binding
CPI books GmbH, Leck

www.degruyter.com

www.ingramcontent.com/pod-product-compliance
Lightning Source LLC
Chambersburg PA
CBHW081103220326
41598CB00038B/7205